JOHN WHITE

EROS DEFILED

THE CHRISTIAN & SEXUAL SIN

Inter-Varsity Press
Downers Grove
Illinois 60515

Other books by John White

The Cost of Commitment
Daring to Draw Near
The Fight
The Golden Cow
The Masks of Melancholy
Parents in Pain

Fantasy by John White

The Tower of Geburah
The Iron Sceptre

© 1977 by Inter-Varsity Christian Fellowship of the United States of America

InterVarsity Press is the book-publishing division of Inter-Varsity Christian Fellowship, a student movement active on campus at hundreds of universities, colleges and schools of nursing. For information about local and regional activities, write IVCF, 233 Langdon St., Madison, WI 53703.

Distributed in Canada through InterVarsity Press, 1875 Leslie St., Unit 10, Don Mills, Ontario M3B 2M5, Canada.

ISBN 0-87784-781-9
Library of Congress Catalog Card Number: 76-39711

Printed in the United States of America

21	20	19	18	17	16	15	14	13	12	11	10	9	8	7
95	94	93	92	91	90	89	88	87	86	85	84	83	82	

TO MY PATIENTS,
WHO HAVE TAUGHT ME TO
LOOK WITH FRESH EYES
ON THE PAINS
AND THE PROBLEMS WROUGHT
BY SEXUAL SIN

CONTENTS

INTRODUCTION

Christians do two things about the sexual failures of their fellow Christians. They denounce the sins and they avoid the sinners. The more offbeat the sin, the greater the horror and the more people shrink back from the man or woman who committed it.

I have no quarrel with denunciation and can understand the avoidance; but things must change. Our reactions too often stem from fears, unconscious fears of our own sexual weaknesses or of our inadequacy to deal with the "sexual" sinner.

I want to help sexual sinners, many of whom come to see me in my practice. I know that for every one I see there are a thousand more who are not being helped. My object in writing is to reach out to this unhappy multitude. Some may find help by reading my book. Others may be helped by you as a result of the new insight you may gain from the book.

Some may buy the book because it combines respectability (it is a "Christian" book) with titillation (what delightful fantasies might not lie between the covers)! Others may feel guilty about buying it. I shall do my best to avoid sexually stimulating passages. My real concern is the loneliness, the misery and the heartaches which so often accompany sexual sin.

Sex within marriage was given that human loneliness might end. "It is not good that the man should be alone" (Gen. 2:18). Reproduction is its secondary not its primary purpose though it is fitting that new life should arise as a result of union and love. Certainly love and closeness between parents are even more important to the healthy growth of children than is the love that each parent may give to the children.

It is then a paradox that what God gave to end human aloneness proves often to cause the very thing it was ordained to abolish—alienation. The alienation is what concerns me. I have no heart to denounce sexual sin for I am too moved by its misery.

Yet I use the word *sin* deliberately. Though I have no heart to denounce them (and am not critical of those who do) I recognize that certain forms of sexual behavior are sinful. It may seem strange that a psychiatrist should talk about sin. Ought I not rather to talk about "deviant sexual behavior," "sexual hang-ups" and "psychiatric illness"? Ought I not to emphasize the reasons why people behave the way they do rather than to adopt an outmoded judgmental stance?

Judgment and Compassion

My stance is not judgmental. To be judgmental means to have a condemning and self-righteous attitude toward someone. I have neither the right nor the desire to look down on men and women involved in sexual sin. At the same time I cannot pretend that morality does not exist. Adultery is sinful. If there are circumstances under which it ceases to be sinful, I do not know about them. It may "feel so beautiful, so *right*," as one of my patients once told me, but this makes no difference. It is sin.

It is at this point that many of us fail to reflect the Spirit of God. We seem incapable of calling something sin without having feelings of condemnation toward the sinner. Or else if we discover within ourselves compassion and understanding for a sinner, we try to forget that his action has been sinful. We need to become compassionate realists.

You can use nonjudgmental language while entertaining a judgmental attitude. You can also use judgmental language without being in the least judgmental.

I remember a psychiatrist friend of mine referring to another psychiatrist and saying, "He's *sick*." Condensed into the two words were a world of disgust and contempt. His tone of voice made the word *sick* mean "dirty, vicious pervert." My friend despised the man he was talking about. In speaking as he did he used a neutral (nonjudgmental) word but entertained a judgmental attitude.

On the other hand Jesus' final word to a cowering, promiscuous woman was, "Go, and do not sin again" (Jn. 8:11). There was no sting in the "judgmental" word *sin*. Both Jesus and the woman knew that what she had done was wrong. Yet the words, "Neither do I condemn you," had already taken the sting away, filling her with hope and joy. If judgmentalism is to be found in the scene, it is to be found in the men who dragged her into the street and whose very spirit of condemnation boomeranged to condemn them just as they had tried to condemn the woman and Jesus. They slunk away damned by their own damning hearts.

Let me then establish a principle. Sexual sin, being sin, calls for repentance from the sinner and forgiveness from God. In addition it calls for compassionate understanding and help from Christians, especially where complex psychological factors are associated with it. Part of the very help psychiatrists, counselors and others may give lies in bringing sexual sinners into an understanding of the depth and reality of God's forgiveness. Nothing so liberates a man from the grip of sin as the intoxicating discovery that he is freely accepted and forgiven. We have an altogether unscriptural fear that easy forgiveness makes a man think lightly of sin. God's forgiveness is not "easy," it cost the death of his Son. It costs the sinner the admission of his own guilt and helplessness. Mediated by the Spirit through a helping brother or sister, *a grasp, a dawning awareness, of that forgiveness sets a man free to be holy.*

But we must be careful while talking about sin not to fall into the trap of feeling that the physical aspect of sex is itself sinful. Even those of us who belong to the older generation know intellectually that it is not. Yet we find it hard to rid ourselves of inner feelings of its uncleanness. Or if not we still condemn ourselves for sexual feelings we experience in our daily lives. Some of us are full of sexual urges, urges with which we wish we did not have to cope. Cravings tingle forcefully in our bodies. Struggling against such cravings, men and women in past ages submitted their bodies to painful lashings or drove them to hard work or starved them to gain control. Often the very measures they used became in their turn perverted forms of sexual gratification. How then can we in the twentieth century, stimulated artificially every day in a score of ways, be in control of our passions?

Pleasure Designed by God

Our first step must be to thank a loving Creator that we experience sexual desire. For not only is physical sex itself ordained by God. The physical pleasures of sex are God-given. Your body has the capacity to be deliciously stimulated because God made it so. Pleasure, as C. S. Lewis once pointed out, is God's invention, not the devil's.

Unfortunately the modern world, like the ancient world before it, has made a goddess of sensuality, worshiping sexual pleasure instead of receiving it with thanksgiving. Men and women have become slaves of lust rather than joy-filled servants of God. And a Christian, reacting to a flagrantly hedonistic culture, may fall into one of two extreme errors. On the one hand he may himself be enslaved and on the other, in his fear of lust, he may deny himself the enjoyment God planned for him.

What should be a Christian's attitude toward sexual pleasure?

A Christian must bear three things in mind, one of which has already been mentioned. First, he must realize that God made his body (including the "sexual" parts of it) and that he equipped it with a nervous system designed to enable each of us to experience exquisite pleasures, pleasures that anticipate the rapture our spirits will one day enjoy in a love-relationship with Christ.

Second, pleasure is a by-product in life, not a goal. A hedonist is someone for whom pleasure is a guiding principle.

Sigmund Freud saw man as a creature whose every action was controlled by the pursuit of pleasure and the avoidance of pain. Most of us have already discovered, however, that when we devote ourselves to pursuing pleasure, pleasure ceases to be a delight. Our appetites grow jaded and require ever more stimulation. On the other hand when we devote our lives to loving obedience to God and to serve one another, we find that the pleasures that eluded us when we made them our goal spring unbidden to surprise us. To seek pleasure is to find disenchantment. To seek God is to find (among other things) piercing pleasures.

Third, sexual pleasure was designed to be enjoyed within marriage. The physical side of sex is only part of a larger whole. I stated at the beginning of this chapter that the first purpose of sex is the ending of isolation and loneliness. And loneliness can only end where trust exists—trust that someone has made a commitment to me and I to that person in a sworn covenant until death parts us. Within such a relationship the physical pleasures of sex may blossom and mysteriously deepen to solidify the relationship. We do not marry in order to copulate. If this were so, marriage would indeed be "legalized prostitution." Marriages founded on physical sex quickly pall. We marry to make an alliance of mutual help and service, and as an expression of love. Intimacy in such a context is the seal of commitment. It is also a delicate communication of love and trust by which a man and a woman know each other ever more deeply.

There would be no need for me to write a book of this kind, however, if all of us were constantly experiencing the kind of rapture I speak of. But many people are not married at all. They are single, divorced or widowed and their craving for what could have been so beautiful has become distorted and troublesome. Others who are married fall far short of the ideal and for various reasons have fallen into sexual practices of which they are ashamed or with which they are bored or disgusted.

Bombarded by erotic stimuli from all sides how can they cope? What should their attitudes be to themselves and their sexuality? How can their sexual experience be integrated into their Christian experience? Where can they find, when burdened by sin and shame, the kind of fellowship which will provide forgiveness and hope? One thing I know is that God reaches out to them and that he wants to reach out through his people. I pray that my book may be a part of that reaching out, a reaching out to cleanse where there is filth, to heal where there is pain and to illumine the dark shadows of loneliness with the light and joy of fellowship.

PART I

SIN, SEX & YOU

1
SEX, SCIENCE AND MORALITY

There are three kinds of questions people ask about sexual behavior. Is it legal? Is it normal? Is it sinful?

The first inquires whether we are allowed to do it or whether we will be in trouble with the police. Prostitution, for instance, is illegal in some places and legal in others. In this book we shall not concern ourselves with the legality of sexual behavior. It is a fascinating side study (for example, until recently, oro-genital sex between husband and wife was illegal in several Canadian provinces) but irrelevant to our main purpose.

The second question asks whether a given form of sexual behavior is "sick," perverted or an evidence of emotional disturbance. Illegal sex is dealt with by policemen and magistrates. Sick sex might call for a psychiatrist or a psychologist.

The third question asks about morality. It may be legal to do something. It may also be normal to do it. But is it right? Fornication (if minors are not involved and the relationship is by mutual consent) is legal in most places. It does not break the law. Most people today would also consider it to be normal (that is, not "queer" or "sick" in any sense). But how are we to decide whether it is right or not?

Science, society (or the law) and religion each has its own evaluation of sexual behavior. In order of strictness science (which considers the normality or abnormality of sexual behavior) is the most liberal and religion the most restricted. Society (or the law) comes somewhere between the two.

Adultery, for example, would be regarded by the behavioral scientist as normal in Western society. The law takes a stricter view. Adultery, while not being a criminal offence, is still grounds for divorce. Society turns a blind eye to adultery so long as nobody protests. But when someone does, his protests are recognized as grounds for legal action. Religion takes the strictest view of all. Most Christian bodies condemn adultery whether anyone protests or not.

The Situation Ethicist and I

In this book I shall have to keep two kinds of questions in mind: the *normality* of sexual behavior and its *morality*.

I accept Holy Scripture as the rule by which morality is judged; but then people who differ with me about right and wrong in sex also appeal to Scripture. It seems to me that many people espouse situation ethics on the basis of Scripture. I might disagree with the way they interpret Scripture, but I cannot brush aside their arguments by simply saying that I believe the Bible. At times I shall have to refer to specific Scriptures and give my reason for interpreting them the way I do.

As I understand it situation ethics demands that we consider more than the action carried out. We must ask under what circumstances it took place and what were the motives of the persons involved.

16

Most of us will agree with this. However, there are some principles of Scripture that seem to be of such paramount importance as to exclude all but the most far-fetched circumstances, and we must try to grasp why. Adultery is one. Circumstances might change the degree of guilt involved, but they can never take it entirely away. Time does not soften the diamond hardness of the rule "Thou shalt not commit adultery" (Ex. 20:14, KJV).

Yet the situational ethicists have done us a service. Many of us in the past, while not accepting the Roman Catholic distinction between venal and mortal sins, have still made unconscious, if not conscious, judgments about the seriousness of different sins. Until recently we have (in evangelical circles) automatically thought of sexual sin as being especially wicked. More than this, we have (perhaps without realizing it) assumed that it is evil, *simply because it is sexual.*

Yet consider the three forms of sexual activity: rape, sexual relations for an afternoon's fun and sexual relations as an expression of deep affection. All may represent fornication, but clearly all are not equally serious. All may be sinful, but not all are equally abhorent.

It is not easy to compare one sin with another for emotional as well as philosophical reasons. We tend both to feel virtuous about sins we are not guilty of and to condemn fiercely weaknesses we are unaware of in ourselves. Thus older evangelical Christians feel that sexual offences call for church discipline, while bitterness, pride and greed for money and power are hardly noticed. Let a man make a million dollars and we may excuse the way he did it and elect him to the church board. But let him go to bed with his neighbor's wife, and the church is buzzing with scandal. Cliquishness and snobbery walk unabashed among us while fiery preachers denounce with unholy glee the latest rise in hemlines or dip in necklines. I know of one church near where I live where the ladies' prayer meeting is felt to have been "spiritual" if it has centered around the scandals of wordly fashions. But let any sister raise the

17

matter of gossip and lack of charity in the church, and she will be regarded as lacking in understanding.

What I say applies to middle-aged rather than to younger Christians. Many of the younger generation of evangelicals, disgusted by what they consider to be cant and hypocrisy in their elders, show an appalling lack of concern about sexual standards—appalling not because of the sins they commit but because, having thrown aside the sexual prejudices of their fathers, they are left without direction in a moral wilderness.

The Risk

Our choice need not lie between narrow prejudice and a moral wilderness. Sex has a purpose given in Scripture—to abolish isolation ("It is not good that the man should be alone" —Gen. 2:18 and see 2:23-25).

Some people choose isolation. They do so not because at heart they prefer isolation but because they fear rejection and estrangement. A human encounter is fraught with fear, the fear that the other will reject and despise me when he discovers what I am. I am torn between the yearning to expose myself and the fear of shame and of another's scorn. I long to cast aside every shred that covers me and be known and loved for my naked self. Yet though I am tired of the many masks I hide behind, the disguises with which I confront the world I live in; though they are burdensome and heavy, concealing the deformities and weaknesses I hate and fear—if I strip them from me, how terrible is the risk I run! Who can assure me that it is safe to do so?

Yet if I do not expose myself, how will I ever discover the wonders of being enfolded by and lost in another?

Erotic pleasure is the most superficial benefit of sex. It is a delight but only the delight of a moment. The bodily exposure that arouses and accompanies it can be both profoundly symbolic and powerfully healing. It symbolizes the uncovering of our inner selves, our deepest fears and yearnings. As I look tenderly on the body of another, as I experience what it is to feel the tenderness of another's caresses and the delight of knowing I am loved as well as loving, it seems momentarily impossible to separate myself from my body. So much am I a bodily creature that the one who accepts my body, caresses also with tenderness my inmost being. Or so at times it seems.

It makes sense then that sexual relations be confined to marriage. For acceptance and mutual disclosure are not the activities of a moment but the delicate fabric of a lifetime's weaving. To assure their development they need the sturdy framework of sworn commitment buttressed by social laws. Some who choose isolation do so from fear of failure. A marriage commitment is assurance against rejection and so allows for full self-disclosure by both partners.

Each time that sexual relations spring from casual encounters, something of their healing and life-giving nature is destroyed. The body is not for fornication nor fornication for the body (see 1 Cor. 6:13-20). God designed us to learn in the body and through the body the intimacy of a close personal relationship. The body is not designed to benefit us from sexual relationships outside commitment. Such relationships enslave and destroy.

The Gold Seal Is Not a Guarantee

You may object and say: What difference does a marriage certificate make? Can a piece of paper change sex from a sin into a wholesome activity?

Of course not. The fact that my wife and I are married does not mean that we invariably do something good and wholesome when we have sex together. It is not in this sense that the bed is undefiled. Either of us can be callous and selfish in our sexual relations. We could even be cruel or sadistic. A marriage certificate does not justify everything that goes on in the marriage bed.

In any case the piece of paper is not what counts. I have no idea where my marriage certificate is right now. As a legal document it never did impress me. The awkward handwriting of the pastor who signed it and its cheap gold seal always looked incongruous and faintly ridiculous in the face of the solemnity of what we were doing.

What I remember is that I swore in the presence of witnesses that only death would prevent me from caring for and nurturing my wife-to-be. I meant that vow. It gave me the right to know my wife by setting the only conditions which made that knowledge a possibility. It was the vow and the lifelong commitment that made the difference, not the piece of paper that bore witness to them. And any knowledge of man by woman or of woman by man that falls short of these conditions, falls short of what God intended sex to be. It is less than and cheaper than the real thing.

I wish it were possible to say that marriage vows guaranteed the realization of the intimacy I write about. Unfortunately vows must be lived out. Many who swear oaths fail to keep them. I do not mean they fail by "being unfaithful" but that they fail in the task of creating the strong yet delicate fabric of an intimate relationship. A lifelong commitment sworn in marriage vows merely makes that relationship possible. It does not guarantee it.

The most basic principle on which to found a sexual ethic lies in the teaching of Christ and his relationship with his bride, the church (Eph. 5:21-33). Can anyone doubt the permanence of that relationship or the importance of the fidelity of both parties?

Therefore I hold that only the sexual activity that takes place between a husband and wife for their mutual comfort and as the process by which they learn communion fulfills God's purpose for sex.

One might ask whether sex is not intended primarily for begetting children. I do not believe so. It is true that God commanded man to be fruitful and multiply, but this represents a goal within marriage, not its primary purpose. And as I mentioned in the introduction, into what better environment

20

could children be born than into the security of a stable affection between their parents? Creation is a fitting product of love. But sexual love in the broadest sense of the term is an end in itself. It does not need procreation to justify it. Procreation might seem the biological purpose of sexual union, but in the divine order of things the creation of a relationship comes first both chronologically and in importance.

As It Was Meant to Be

So much for morality. But what of normality? How do we decide what is normal sex and what constitutes sick or perverted sex?

If we are to be guided by Scripture, the normal is whatever fulfills God's purpose in designing something. So any sex which fails to conform to his purpose must be abnormal. But what has science to say?

Science supplies questions rather than answers. Science can tell us what is *usual or average* in sexual behavior. It can also tell us how our bodies and emotions work. Science is descriptive. It seeks to explore the designs of the Master Designer.

One does not need to be well grounded in science, however, to see what stares us in the face. Today in our feverish pursuit of sensual pleasure we are rediscovering a broad range of erotic pleasures which have flourished as each civilization has entered into its phase of decadence. Christian couples are enjoying such delights as oro-genital sex. A penis is caressed by lips and a tongue or a tongue massages the clitoris, vagina or the nipples. Is such sex normal?

All science can say is that it is "a statistical norm," that is, that the majority of people do it. *Normal* and *average* do not mean the same thing, however. When a Christian talks about something being normal, he is talking about it being "as it was meant to be." The scientist, on the other hand, knows nothing of meaning or purpose. He can only describe what he sees. And to him the normal means "the way things are" not the way they should be.

Yet common sense tells us that the vagina is better adapted to accommodate the penis than either the mouth or the rectum. And if the hand and glove relationship of penis and vagina were not enough, there is still the functional relationship between them. Procreation may be a secondary purpose of sex, but it is still a purpose, and no woman yet conceived a baby between her teeth.

What am I saying? Is oro-genital sex abnormal? Is it wrong? Are all the many varieties of sexual stimulation also wrong? To all of these questions I can give no simple answer. And even if I did, the answers would not be important. What is important is that any form of erotic stimulation which is not part of an ongoing sexual relationship, and which does not lead to sexual intercourse between a man and a woman, however normal it may be in the statistical sense, is subnormal from the Christian standpoint.

I choose the word subnormal deliberately. Erotic stimulation without intercourse is like the pacifier without the bottle or like a diet of chocolate candy and liqueurs—delightful as part of a whole but intoxicating and sickening when taken alone.

We could spend much longer on the moral and scientific guidelines to sexual behavior. The subject is a vast one and I shall say more as we come to specific patterns. But my purpose at this point is not to give instruction in ethics so much as to help people in distress. Knowing what is sexually right and doing it are two different things. It is time I turned to the practical problems of people caught between their consciences and their relentless urges.

2
YOUR URGES & HOW YOU EXPERIENCE THEM

Your physical needs are controlled by delicate built-in mechanisms. Your breathing, for instance, runs on automatic most of the time. Sensors in your brain detect how much carbon dioxide and oxygen the red cells are carrying and send a stream of messages both to the breath-control centers and to the centers that control your heart's action. If your cells carry too much carbon dioxide, you will begin to breathe more rapidly. If the concentration increases further (say when you climb a steep hill), you slowly become aware that you feel breathless. You notice that you are panting and that your heart is beating hard. Once the carbon dioxide levels are back to normal again, your palpitation and panting stop.

If you want to experiment with the control mechanisms, try overbreathing. Breathe in and out as deeply and as quickly as you can twenty times. (Make sure you lie down first. You may get quite dizzy.) You will notice that you have no particular urge to go on breathing for a minute or so. The carbon dioxide has been "washed out" of your blood and the control mechanism has switched you on to a "no breathe" cycle until the level of carbon dioxide begins to rise again. But notice too what has happened to you consciously. God has so designed the working of your body that you *want* to do what you *need* to do.

A Tall, Frosted Glass of Orange Juice

Your need for water is controlled in the same way as your need for air. Think of going on a long, hard walk on a hot, dusty day. The sun beats down. You are sweating hard and your mouth is dry. As you come into the house, flop into a chair in the kitchen craving a drink, you see a tall glass of orange juice, misty with condensation on the glass. The glass seems irresistible, and you reach to grasp its cold surface and start drinking. Your lips, tongue and throat relish the cold liquid as it flows past them. You may even hunt in the refrigerator for more juice and drink another glass.

How do you feel? If you are like most people, you will heave a sigh of contentment, murmuring as you relax in your chair, "Man, did that ever taste good!"

But let us suppose that you have not been on a long walk on a hot, dusty day. Let us suppose, instead, that your doctor has ordered you to take extra fluids and that you have been drinking glass after glass of juices, tea, coffee, milk all day. As you view yet another large drink you find that you experience distaste at the thought of downing yet another glass.

What has happened? In the first instance your body's supply of water had been depleted. Tiny brain cells in your hypothalamus and pituitary gland had taken note of the fact and issued instructions to your kidneys (telling them to conserve your water supply and use less for the manufacture of urine) and to your salivary glands telling them to hold back

24

on water for saliva. At the same time you became conscious of discomfort. Your mouth felt dry and hot and you "felt thirsty." The longer you were kept without fluid, the worse you would feel until your craving for liquid became intolerable. At that point you would do almost anything to get hold of water. Once again you *want* to do what you *need* to do and the greater your need the greater your want.

But notice what we are saying. God could have devised some other means whereby our need for water was met. But he chose to do so *by giving us pleasure from drinking*. He designed life to be maintained by built-in pleasures.

We notice then that for each of our bodily functions we experience a sort of cycle, though we may not be fully aware of what is happening because we are so used to collaborating with our control mechanisms. When we are deprived of either air or water, however, the cycle becomes more pronounced. We can represent it as follows:

Preliminary Phase	*Phase I*	*Phase II*	*Phase III*
Restlessness⟶	Agitation⟶	Alleviation⟶	Relaxation and Relief
(Mild desire to drink or to breathe deeply)	*(Intense thirst or feelings of suffocation)*	*(Drinking or breathing deeply)*	*(Loss of desire to drink or to breathe deeply)*

Not all bodily needs are served in precisely the same way, but there are similarities. Let me take another example. I remember once sitting in a long diagnostic conference drinking cup after cup of coffee. After an hour or so I began to feel uneasy. I wished people would hurry the conference along faster. I was restless and fidgety in my chair. Suddenly it dawned on me that I felt the way I did because I needed to go to the washroom. My control centers had been signalling furiously, but at first I hadn't noticed.

I excused myself. Once out of the conference room my pace quickened. To my great relief the washroom door was unlocked. A few minutes later all my tension and restlessness had melted away as if by magic. I was conscious only of a sense of peace and I sighed contentedly.

Again you can see how the cycle works—restlessness → agitation → alleviation → feelings of relaxation and relief. And as I said before, I wanted to do what I *needed* to do. My sense of relief was a very real pleasure.

Appetites and Attitudes

Some psychologists and psychiatrists refer to these mechanisms I have described as *drives*, but the term is a technical one connected with disputed theories and I will avoid it. I shall use the word *urge* by which I mean simply, "the subjective longing to do something." So far we have discussed our respiration urges, our thirst urges and our urge to pass urine. Similarly we could discuss the urge to eat or any number of urges including sexual urges.

Scientists offer a number of different theories to explain the facts I have been describing, but we need not concern ourselves at this point with them. All we need to do is to observe how our physical appetites affect us in our daily living.

We have noticed a law governing our urges: They are not steady things; we experience cyclical phases in their operation; God has placed within our bodies mechanisms to assure that our physical needs are met. Restlessness, desire and an urge to do or get whatever is necessary are all created within us to assure us of life and health. And as our needs are met, we learn from experience how pleasant and contented we feel when the necessary adjustments (intake of food, water, air or expulsion of waste matter) have been made.

Sigmund Freud, as I mentioned earlier, referred to these adjustments of body needs by our craving and our satisfactions as the *pleasure-pain principle*. God gave us pleasure and pain to promote our physical health. Freud was correct in pointing out that pleasure pulls and that pain pushes, but wrong in assuming that his pleasure-pain principle is all that is required to explain human behavior. The principle may guide us but it does not control us.

We are not always conscious of the operation of our physical cycles for our minds are occupied with other matters. My children do not notice they are hungry when they are excited by a game of softball. When I call them in to dinner they say, quite sincerely, "But daddy, I'm not hungry." Nevertheless, ten minutes later they are polishing off large quantities of food and asking for more. The hunger cycle was operating, but they only became aware of it when their attention was taken away from softball and centered on the mouth-watering visions and smells of a freshly cooked meal.

Similarly it was the frosted glass of orange juice that suddenly made you aware of how thirsty you were after your walk on a hot day. For the same reason the closer I got to the washroom, the more urgently I felt my need to hurry.

We discover, then, another law. When we are in the "need" phase of our physiological cycles, the sight, sound or thought of something that could meet our need has the effect of adding an urgency to it. The need, in the presence of the supply, becomes almost unbearable. It is for this reason that ancient torturers would torment thirsty men by placing water just out of their reach.

God sometimes makes provision for unbearable urges. Our minds may be seized by competing interests that block our urges. This is especially noticeable in relation to food and to sex. Only when life is threatened does the craving become unblockable. I pointed out, for instance, that my children forgot their hunger when they were excited by a game of softball. As we explore the matter further it becomes more interesting yet.

Let's suppose I am sitting in my office in the late afternoon and my hunger cycle is in the need phase. My stomach is empty, my blood sugar is down, and a whole series of data are being fed into the control centers in a part of my brain called the hypothalamus with the message, "Food is needed." However, other messages marked, "Top priority," are being fed into the computer of my mind. So I am not aware of hunger.

Suddenly something makes me think of a medium rare T-bone steak. Somehow from inside me an image of steak obtrudes itself. It dances before my eyes. My brain begins to smell what my nose doesn't. My mouth waters and suddenly the vision of steak makes me aware of how hungry I am.

Sexual Fasting

Starving people can be in one of two states. Some experience hunger as torture. They fight, steal, even kill to get food. Others experience no hunger at all.

It depends upon the attitude (or mindset) of the starving person. If, for instance, I decide voluntarily to fast, I will experience hunger for a couple of days and then suddenly a strange absence of hunger. If, on the other hand, I have no wish to fast and you deprive me of food, I will spend my days drooling over visions of it and my nights dreaming about it. My hunger will grow intolerable.

In many ways sex urges differ little from hunger urges. Many a husband will say to his wife, "Honey, I don't know what's the matter with me. I feel sort of—I don't know how I feel—sort of restless." With a secret smile his wife may reply, "I think I know what you need." Later, in the darkness as they lie side by side in peaceful relaxation and contentment, he may say, "Yes, I guess you *did* know what I needed."

But what of single men and women and of all those for whom the hungers of sex cannot be satisfied? What of those who twist and turn in restless half sleep haunted by fantasies that mock and inflame them?

There *is* such a thing as sexual fasting. Many people, I am well aware, are not able to find it, but it exists.

Just as the fasting person finds he no longer wishes for food while the starving person is tortured by mental visions of it, so some are able to experience the peace of sexual abstinence when they need to. Others are tormented. Everything depends upon their mindset or attitude. The slightest degree of ambivalence or double-mindedness spells ruin.

I cannot stress this principle enough. Neither hunger for food nor hunger for sex increase automatically until we explode into uncontrollable behavior. Rather it is as though a spring is wound up, locked in place, ready to be released when the occasion arises. And should that occasion not arise (and here I refer especially to sex), *I need experience no discomfort.*

Under appropriate circumstances the cycle may be arrested at a stage of tension. In normal married living it may endlessly repeat itself. Following the sexual climax of intercourse there is peace and relaxation. Although some couples pride themselves in their capacity to achieve multiple orgasms, most men and women find that physical passion has given place to a contentment in their physical closeness and to no further desire. At that point there is little capacity for further stimulation. The cycle is complete.

But as the hours lengthen into days, tension slowly rises. And if during a time of tension a sexually erotic scene, a physically attractive person of the opposite sex, a chance brushing of hands or one of a hundred other stimuli arouses us, we are made painfully aware that we are full of sexual feelings.

At such times what God intended to be a delight can become a raging torment. How that torment affects us, what specific temptations it flings in our faces will depend upon our nature and our past experiences. Many Christian men and women are ashamed of their failures. Others cover their shame with defiance. Some grow bitter and cynical about the power of Christ and wonder at his failure to deliver them. Others dabble in sexual dreariness and declare that it is beautiful. It is to all such that I devote the chapters that follow.

PART II

SEXUAL SINS

3
SEX ON A DESERT ISLAND

$\mathbf{M}$asturbating is stimulating yourself sexually by manipulating your sexual organs. Infants and young children may (or may not) stop short of orgasm (sexual climax). From puberty onward masturbation proceeds to orgasm with increasing frequency.

There are many techniques, some involving the use of clothing, mirrors and self-inflicted pain. The weirder the technique, the "sicker" the sex. There are masochistic, suicidal rituals chosen because of the erotic ecstacy that is experienced at the point of death.

I see no point in describing techniques. Many I have come across in my practice are pitiful testimonials to frustrated longing and loneliness.

People masturbate from childhood to old age. Married men and women, single men and women, widows, widowers, divorced people, homosexuals, heterosexuals, clergy and laity are found among the ranks of masturbators.

Security in Numbers

No one really knows how many people masturbate regularly. Kinsey, who startled the world with his studies a number of years ago, said that almost all men have at times practiced masturbation. Other studies show that a high proportion of men continue to practice it at least periodically all their lives. The percentage of women was lower, according to Kinsey.[1] His much-criticized study was the first of many all of which tend to confirm and in some cases to extend his findings.

How can anyone be sure of figures? It might be argued that the people who volunteer for a study about sex must already have sexual hang-ups. (Why else should they volunteer?) If so, Kinsey had what statisticians call a "biased sample" of the general population making his figures too high. On the other hand it could also be argued that fear of self-disclosure would keep other people from collaborating. For every show-off who wants to parade his sex life there may be a guilt-ridden moralist who wants to hide his.

Why are statistics important? If you are bothered about your masturbation, you may find it reassuring to discover that you are in good company. I suspect most people's interest in sex statistics is of this kind. Should this be your worry, the accuracy of Kinsey's figures matters little. One thing is certain: Lots of people masturbate. As Dearborn puts it, "No other form of sexual activity has been so frequently discussed, so roundly condemned, and more universally practiced, than masturbation."[2]

The onset of mental illness is sometimes accompanied by an increased frequency of masturbation. It is not true that masturbation causes mental illness. Its increasing frequency seems to be a result rather than a cause of some forms of early schizophrenia. Early in depressive illness it may either increase or decrease in frequency.

People who are anxious and lonely have recourse to it though it affords them scant solace. Children who are under stress at home, adolescents in turmoil, husbands whose wives are pregnant, and men and women away from home all tend to masturbate. Some people masturbate to get to sleep, others because they feel depressed or inadequate.

Life on the Island
How should Christians view masturbation?

Old-time preachers condemned it as dangerous and wicked. Young people were warned of its disastrous consequences, a warning that did not prevent them from practicing it but that did lead to anxiety and a deep sense of guilt. Yet nowadays many Christian adolescents masturbate with no feelings of guilt. They are taught that sexual tension is inevitable and that masturbation is nature's way of alleviating it. We might almost coin the dictum: It is better to masturbate than to burn.

I am glad that the younger generation has been relieved of a burden of guilt and fear that once haunted so many of us. Some people have become obsessed with the struggle against masturbation. They have prayed and fasted, have wept and "trusted God for victory." They have "yielded to the Holy Spirit." They have tried physical exercise, "wholesome activities" and early morning devotions. Sometimes they have been elated in finding "victory" only to be cast down later to find themselves masturbating again.

As with any addiction there seems to be a struggle between two parts of the struggler, the one yearning for sexual excitement and the other for deliverance. And the yearning for deliverance wanes as the yearning for sexual excitement grows stronger.

What are we to say? Is masturbation right or wrong?

If you yourself masturbate, there are a couple of things you should know at once. First of all, you do not *have* to go on masturbating. Nothing terrible will happen to you if you stop. It is not true that sexual urges, like steam pressure inside a boiler, will explode when the pressure reaches a certain point.

You may object, however, and tell me that my theory is very fine but that your experience suggests the exact opposite. "At some points *I just can't help it*," you tell me. "The tension is too great." Fine. I accept what you say. This is indeed how you feel. But your body is fooling you.

Nor am I saying, "You don't have to masturbate, so stop right now!" I know that in experience it is far from being so simple. Later I hope to give some guidelines which may help. All I am saying for the moment is that you are not the helpless victim of uncontrollable urges however strongly you may feel the contrary. You are responsible for your actions.

My second point is a reminder of what sex is all about. Its primary purpose is to end aloneness. It is a physical girder which two people whose flesh has become one use to help build the house of a solid relationship. Behind the very feelings that torture you lies a longing to know and to be known, to love and to be loved. Indeed the Elizabethan word for sexual intercourse is "to know" a man or woman.

This is one of the reasons that masturbation never really satisfies. Orgasm is a small part of a greater and more personal whole. You may not (as John Donne affirms) *be* an island, yet in a sense you are living on an island alone. Your sexual longings are associated with a deeper need—that someone should share your island and bring your isolation to an end. You are frustrated as you pace its length and breadth. The empty seas are about you, and the breakers crash lifelessly upon the sand. Your eyes ache for the sight of smoke on the horizon, and your ears ache for the music of human speech. Masturbation is to be alone on an island. It frustrates the very instinct it gratifies.

But having said that, there is not much else to say. Nowhere in Scripture is masturbation mentioned. Catholics used to condemn masturbation as onanism, after Onan (Gen. 38: 4-10) who "spilled [his] semen on the ground."

Onan did not masturbate. He had sexual intercourse with his brother's widow, the type of intercourse known as coitus interruptus. The reason God was displeased with Onan was not that the practice of coitus interruptus in itself displeased him but that Onan's aim in spilling his seed on the ground was to avoid siring children in his brother's name. It was the motive, not the act, that was condemned. Any children born of his brother's widow, sired by Onan, would have been regarded as the children of Onan's dead brother. The whole problem with the official Catholic view of sex is that it over emphasizes procreation and undervalues sex as communion.

Masturbation is autostimulation, not sexual stimulation by another person. It is an intrapersonal not an interpersonal affair. Its defect lies at this very point: It takes what was meant to be a powerful urge encouraging a close personal relationship but aborts it. That which was meant to be shared is squandered in solitude. But sad and depressing as this may be, it can hardly account for the crushing guilt that some people suffer. How then can we explain the sense of guilt?

Origins of Guilt

Theories differ. Freudian psychoanalysis suggests that masturbation is linked with "unconscious incestuous fantasies." The oedipus theory has never been firmly entrenched among leading psychoanalytic thinkers, and there is now a growing movement among them to play down the theory in the face of anthropological and experimental evidence.[3] Yet so firmly does it remain a part of popular psychoanalytic and lay thinking, that we should perhaps have a look at it.

In the oedipal phase of psychosexual development (from the ages of four to six), boys are said to have desires to possess their mothers and to supplant their fathers. Girls have similar wishes toward their fathers.

Let us consider what happens to the girl according to analytic theory. To possess her father she must supplant her mother. Aware of this in some dim way she begins to see mother as a formidable adversary, infinitely more powerful than herself. Moreover she longs to enjoy the shelter and understanding of her mother. Her need for her mother's protection combined with her fear of her usually force the girl to give up her ambition to win first place in her father's affections. Instead she decides to become like mother and to take second place in daddy's love.

The boy, on the other hand, is said to have an incestuous wish to possess his mother. He sees an opponent in his father. All his life he has known him as the ultimate authority, the giver of laws. But in the nature of things the boy, too, must make a compromise.

To do so, like his sister, he uses two so-called *defense mechanisms*—psychological mechanisms used to keep his fear of his rival (his father) at bay. He incorporates his father and he identifies with him. He takes his father into his own being, as it were, absorbing his image into his soul. Whereas until this point in his life, his father's command has sounded from outside him, it now begins to sound from within. Up to this time he has not understood right and wrong. True, he has understood that certain things made his parents angry. So he would feel anxious when doing them. But now there is a difference. The words, "You mustn't," become, "I mustn't." Conscience or "superego" is born, and to the extent to which the father has been harsh and punitive, to that same extent will the boy's superego be harsh and punitive. His concept of God (thought of as an extension of his own father) will likewise be harsh and punitive.[4]

It is impossible to make sense of analytic theory unless you understand one concept more—the concept of the unconscious. Deep within us all there is said to lie a subterranean cavern where our fiercest urges and our most frightening and shameful memories lie dormant. We are unconscious of them precisely for this reason—they are frightening. But like demons trapped within us they strive to be released and to express themselves.

Among such wishes and memories are those of possessing physically the parent of the opposite sex. The very fact that we hasten so angrily to pour scorn on the thought of our having had sexual desires toward one of our parents is to the analyst a further confirmation of their existence. Our anger, he tells us, is to convince ourselves. We ridicule the theory because it awakens fear within us, fear that what is so deeply buried will rear its head from the grave and leer at us.

If Freud were right, it would make sense that some people feel guilty when they masturbate. For if masturbation were indeed linked in our minds with our incestuous desires, so that these very desires were to rattle their chains in the dungeon to which we have banished them, then masturbation would inevitably be a potent awakener of guilty fear.

The weakness of the analytic view is that so many young people nowadays, like people in certain primitive cultures, masturbate with little or no inner conflict. How do we explain their freedom from guilt feelings? If they, like the rest of us, have incestuous skeletons in their cupboards, why do the skeletons not rattle? The Freudian theory digs deep but either not deep enough or else too deep. It tries to explain guilt but not its absence.

Perhaps a simpler view may be more helpful. John and Nancy might have been reared in homes where sex is the Great Unmentionable. By a thousand small cues they were taught that it was dirty, not to be talked about. They discovered that their sexual organs were not to be played with or exposed. ("Shame on you! That's a dreadful thing to do!" "Put it away or I'll take a pair of scissors and cut it off!" "Don't play with yourself. Nice girls don't do that!" And so on and so on.) Then, denied in pubescence and adolescence any reassurance that sexuality was in fact wholesome and that their sexual feelings were evidence that they were becoming men and women, they naturally feel guilty when they masturbate. Disgust and shame are caught as well as taught.

Many people who ask me for help do not want reassurance,

however. They want to quit masturbating. Why is it so hard to
do?

A Buzzer, a Lever, an Electrode

Of the many theories explaining the grip of habit, perhaps the
easiest to understand are those of behavioral psychology. Behavioral psychology began in modern times with the Russian
physiologist, Ivan Pavlov.[5] Pavlov taught dogs to make their
mouths water at the sound of a buzzer. Every time the buzzer
sounded, meat was brought in to the dog. Soon the dog would
begin to salivate a moment or two after the buzzer sounded.
Even if no meat was brought to the dog, the sound of the buzzer, for a limited number of times, continued to cause the dog
to salivate. Somewhere in the dog's nervous system a *connection* had been made between the buzzer and salivating. He had
been *conditioned* to salivate to a buzzer. The fact that a connect-
ing link had been forged gives rise to the term *connectionism*—a
brand of theories about learning which has many forms and
which dates back as far as Aristotle.

Perhaps the most prevalent form of connectionism in the
West is what is known as *operant conditioning* (a type that B. F.
Skinner is recommending should be applied to the whole human race as an attempt to solve world problems). Operant
conditioning works as follows.

Picture a pigeon in a small box. Picture also a lever sticking
out from the wall of the box. It connects with a mechanism
that releases corn into the box whenever the lever is tripped.

The pigeon moves around the box, stands, moves again,
poking its head here and there as pigeons do. Sooner or later
it trips the lever and the corn falls into the box. At first the
pigeon seems to have made no connection between the lever-
pecking and the corn. But once the same sequence (lever-
pecking—appearance of corn) has occurred several times, the
pigeon begins to peck the bar more frequently. The *reward* of
corn has "stamped into" its nervous system the lesson of how
to trip the lever.[6]

We are now in a position to understand how behaviorists see the grip of habit. They would not call it habit, perhaps, but a "learned pattern of behavior" which was "repetitive." For behaviorists are not trying to tell us that the pigeon says, "Aha! Every time I trip the lever, corn comes. I must trip the lever more frequently!" Nor, "Tripping the lever is becoming a habit. I must quit, I am getting too fat." Behaviorists are not interested in conscious thought. As they see it the pigeon has been programmed to trip levers. It is as though the bird were a kind of computer, automatically doing whatever the programmer made it do. Its behavior has been shaped by rewarding lever-tripping and by not rewarding other kinds of behavior.

Rewards can shape behavior very powerfully. One day, as James Olds of Montreal was placing microelectrodes in the brain of a rat, he made an astonishing discovery. A lever in the box was wired to activate the electrode stimulating a part of the brain. The rat quickly learned to stimulate its own brain. But the remarkable discovery was that so rewarding was lever-tripping that the rat went on tripping it thousands of times in succession. It ceased to do so only when it fell on its side, exhausted. As soon as it recovered, it eagerly went back to the task.

The tip of the electrode rested in a part of the brain just in front of what is called the hypothalamus.[7] This tiny area seemed to specialize in creating wonderful feelings in the rat.

Just what the rat experiences, we do not know. Olds called the area a *reward center*. The brain fibers at that point are connected to centers controlling such things as sex, feeding and sleeping. It is possible that each time the rat tripped the lever, he momentarily felt the rat equivalent of eating medium rare steak, having an orgasm, smelling attar of roses, listening to Beethoven's Ninth and floating on a cloud—all at one time. Whatever the experience, the reward was powerful enough after a few presses of the lever to hook the rat for good. He had what we would call a powerful *lever-addiction*.

According to behaviorists of connectionist schools, masturbation is no different from any other pattern of learned behavior. The learning is deeply ingrained. Because of the erotic pleasure that rewards him, the masturbator *has programmed himself to masturbate*. His personal decisions about masturbating are neither here nor there. He will go on masturbating just as the rat goes on pressing the lever, *unless he is reprogrammed* (that is, programmed not to masturbate).

I have some experience (though perhaps not enough) in conditioning or "programming" human behavior, and while space does not permit me to go into details, I would say that a program designed to extinguish masturbation would have to be so elaborate and time-consuming as to be impractical to carry out.

But do either behaviorism or psychoanalysis give a full explanation of the grip certain habits have on us? If they do, not only is the outlook gloomy for masturbation but for all mankind.

Is man a computor? Is he a rat in a box? Some parts of our behavior *are* automatic, or we could not spare thought for creative activity. If every moment of my existence I had to keep my respiration rate at twenty breaths a minute and my heart rate at eighty and my body temperature at 98°F, much of my mental activity would be taken up with staying alive.

But my breathing is switched to automatic most of the time. I can take over and slow it down or speed it up, but I rarely bother. Most of my daily activities (like walking, climbing stairs, driving a car) are either automatic or semiautomatic. But I can take over at any time. I am like an expensive sports car that can both shift gears manually and run on automatic. The difference is that my mechanisms are more elaborate than the car's.

Behaviorists and analysts go a long way toward explaining the grip of habit, but they do not understand that man, made in the image of God, is a responsible being. They ignore human freedom. In fact their basic assumption is that there is no freedom. In addition they leave many questions unanswered (such as, Why does sexual intercourse slowly decrease in frequency over the years when by their arguments we should be practicing it more and more frequently since it is so powerfully reinforced?).

Some Practical Counsel
Let me begin to draw together some of the threads.

Masturbation is not a good thing, but neither is it a heinous sin. I know I contradict modern educators in hinting that there might be something wrong with it, but there is. I would be less than truthful if I denied it. Anyone who has experienced both sexual intercourse and masturbation knows that there is a dimension of experience in intercourse that is totally lacking in masturbation. That dimension cannot be replaced by masturbation plus fantasies about one's wife, by having sex with a mannikin or by using a synthetic penis. Gadgets and fantasies are not persons but lifeless human creations. Intercourse is with a person who feels, loves and experiences in the way I do. *And when the interpersonal is lacking, sexual stimulation is promoting the very thing it was designed to overcome.*

The modern urge to reassure ourselves that masturbation is fine in moderation springs from a laudable wish to alleviate the excessive fear and guilt it causes many people. With this wish I sympathize. But I must not in my efforts to alleviate guilt say that pale shades of gray are white.

There is also truth in what behaviorists say. The more deeply the erotic pleasure stamps in a masturbatory behavior pattern, the more difficult the pattern will be to erase. Other psychological mechanisms described by other schools of thought could also be cited to explain the grip the habit has. But why bother? Anyone who tries to quit knows how hard it is.

The toughest problem is the spiritual one: Why does God fail to answer my prayer for deliverance when I have trusted him with all my heart? For God does deliver some people (at least they tell us so). And if them why not me? Am I less spiritual than they? What is lacking in the quality of my faith? Many Christians bitterly conclude that since God can't be at fault, they themselves must be.

Earlier in this chapter I mentioned that I know no references to masturbation in Scripture. From this I take it that other matters must cause God more concern than masturbation. Certainly if we go by volume of words, then those sins which hurt and wound others (theft, adultery, violence, desertion, cruelty) and those that mock God (unbelief, rebellion, bitterness) come high on his list.

It is important that in aiming at holiness we bear two forgotten principles in mind. The first is that nowhere does Scripture tell us to *try* to do something or *to do our very best not* to do something else. "Thou shalt . . ." or "Thou shalt not . . ." are the uncompromising expressions used.

The second principle ties in with the first. God has his own program for reshaping our lives. No exact hierarchy of sins or virtues is laid down in Scripture though general principles can be observed. In dealing with you and me, God is doing what we do ourselves when we try to untangle a knotted tangle of string. Certain knots have to wait until other tangles are straightened.

If I am sensitive to the Holy Spirit in my daily walk, I will discover that it is perfectly possible to obey God. It may be painful to do so, but it is always possible. For instance, God may be dealing with me on the issue of forgiveness and be making me aware of my resentment towards my wife. I may not *want* to forgive. But if I want to, I can. To say to me, "Now *try* to forgive her," only gives me an out—"But I *have* tried and I can't." God says: "Forgive!" And though I may hate to, I *can*.

We are never justified in committing sin, but God deals with things one at a time in our lives. There is some thing he is dealing with at the moment in mine. There is no question as to whether I *can* obey or not. When God puts his finger on something, I can.

This is not to say I live sinlessly. I know that he will never cease to throw his spotlight onto things in my life that displease him.

But I have my own priorities. Certain weaknesses humiliate me, and I wish that God would deal with them first. Both of us are grieved by my humiliating defeats. Yet I find that whenever I bring my humiliations to God in prayer, he seems to say: "I know. It grieves me too. But there is something you seem to be avoiding, something you could deal with now if you wanted to. Are you willing to obey me in this—today?" Always the issue he wants me to deal with is one I haggle over and resist him on. But always it is the one in which I *can* and *must* give way to him.

So to you who are frustrated about masturbation I would say the following:

1. God is well able to deliver you. If he isn't doing so at the moment, he may, incredible though it may seem to you, have a prior concern with something else in your life.

2. Your view of the seriousness of your problem is exaggerated. If you search the Scriptures, you will find a lot about virtues God commends to you and sins he warns you about. How do you measure up to them? How about forgetting *your* problem and taking the commands of Scripture seriously? You hurt no one but yourself by masturbating, but whom have you hurt this week by your sarcasm, your coldness, your forgetfulness, your laziness, your lack of tact and courtesy? How many minutes have you praised God in the last twenty-four hours?

3. Thank God for all your sexual feelings. Don't hate them. They may be as difficult to manage as an unbroken horse, but they represent one of God's richest gifts to you. He made you to feel sexual desire. Be glad and rejoice in it. Thank him, too, for the day when you will be master of your sexual drives. Though it tarry, it will come, if you let God be master in other areas in your life.

4. Quit hating yourself. Refuse to listen to the endlessly

torturous accusations of the accuser of the brethren, who accuses you day and night (Rev. 12:10). If you are cast down, God waits for you with wide-open arms. By all means groan, but take your shame to the throne of grace where blood will wash it away. Your will is being freed and will be freed from the grip of masturbation, too, one day. So learn to laugh at your chains, in faith.

5. Refuse to let masturbation cause you discouragement and self-disgust. Thomas R. Kelly said, "Humility does not rest... upon bafflement and discouragement and self-disgust at our shabby lives, a brow-beaten, dog-slinking attitude. It rests upon the disclosure of the consummate wonder of God."[8] He also says "When you catch yourself again, *lose no time in self-recriminations,* but breathe a silent prayer for forgiveness and begin again, just where you are. Offer *this* broken worship up to Him and say: 'This is what I am except Thou aid me.' Admit no discouragement, but ever return quietly to Him and wait in His Presence."[9]

This is what we are, except he aid us. He knows it. We know it. Acknowledging it is the first step to a true walk with God in any area of our lives. As we turn to look at graver sexual sins, as well as petty ones, honesty with ourselves, with God and at times with one another will be a step towards health and spiritual growth.

4
THE FREEDOM THAT ENSLAVES

Our standards are influenced more than we realize by the moral climate we live in. Books have been explicitly sexual for decades. Naked men and women (in full color, and in suggestive postures) seduce our eyes to magazines in drug stores, newsstands and supermarkets. Sexual practices are explicitly acted out, not only in cheap blue movies, but now in more serious films. Nudity, suggestive and symbolic sexuality have been for some years common on stage both in revues and in experimental ballet. Forty years ago we were still saying that paintings and statues of nudes were justified by the artistic integrity of the painter or sculptor. Now we are arguing that sex acts of every variety, being an integral part of life, may become an integral part of all forms of artistic expression.

Nobody really knows how sex's bold conquest of literature,

films and stage relates to changing sexual attitudes. At best the sociologists' explanations are partial. But censorship standards fall as human standards change, and the changes in human and sexual standards engulf us all. In them we live and move and have our being. We are saturated with sexual stimulation, sexual attitudes and new philosophies. Whatever standards we thought we had are shifting uneasily on their shaky foundations.

Swallowing Camels

The church's response to the changed morality has been a mixture of fierce (but hollow) indignation and feeble me-tooism. Some of us preachers have missed the heart of the biblical issues. Others have made concessions which represent a non-Christian compromise. Young and old alike, caught in crosscurrents of uncertainty and driven by passions that do not conveniently subside when confusion arises, have been groping pitifully for help.

Sexual morality can be compared with a building. We have failed by not laying adequate biblical foundations on which it may stand secure. Consequently as storms batter our morality, the walls of the building begin to crumble. At such a time the last thing we need is a moral face-lift which is all most conservative preaching offers. We need to work desperately on what the Bible shows to be the basis of morality. We need a solid foundation.

As for the me-tooism of the new morality, we must be clear from the outset that morality is never "new." It has its roots in the eternal, unchanging nature of God. Like him, real morality cannot have adjectives like *new*, or *old* attached to it. It is ageless.

People have lost confidence in the standards of the church for many reasons. Familiarity with sex has changed their perspective. Thirty years ago high-school sex was sufficiently unusual to be a topic for spicy gossip or vicarious boasting. Now it is so common that high schoolers and junior college students grow troubled about their normality if they are virgins. Slowly, even among Christian young people, the inarticulate feeling is gaining ground that sexual relations should not be condemned between couples who are serious about each other.

It began with the explicit sentiment that we must not condemn non-Christians for their sexual standards. But once you admit so much, it is a short step to adopt the same standards for your own behavior.

Whether the new morality of a few years back has helped to bring this state of affairs about or whether the new morality was itself an excuse to do what people were already doing is anybody's guess. But certainly the feeling is growing that traditional sexual standards of evangelical churches are hypocritical and false. "Sincerity" and "honesty" are the new criteria by which sexual standards are measured.

There may be good, however, in what appears to be a sad and confusing state of affairs. For one thing no one can accuse evangelicals of failing to point to scriptural standards. We may not have built proper foundations, but we have shown what the superstructure should look like. "Fornication and indecency of any kind . . . must not be so much as mentioned among you, as befits the people of God" (Eph. 5:3, NEB). The standard is clear and evangelicals have rightly proclaimed it.

One way we have failed, though, is in our lack of a sense of proportion. Our obsession with sexual purity is out of all proportion to our concern for other Christian virtues. We have strained at gnats and swallowed camels. For though it is true that neither a gnat nor a camel is meant to be swallowed, our failure to condemn with greater zeal sins like avarice, malice, resentment, pride and lying, all of which are found among us, has made our obsession with sexual purity suspect.

Are we really so virtuous? As I take an honest look back at my own life, I can't be proud of the virginity I brought to marriage. It was a feeble thing, bolstered by fears, taboos and ignorance. It had no clear basis in my understanding of Scripture and did not rise naturally from my convictions about the underlying biblical principles. I doubt that I am unique in this respect.

The Guilty Generation

The blame for the moral confusion must be laid at the feet of Christians on both sides of the generation gap. The older generation created the ethical vacuum which demanded a situation ethic. And the younger generation seized on a situation ethic to justify its wrong actions.

By emphasis on the letter of the law, by preoccupation with the details of external behavior (movies, smoking, dancing), by straining at the theological gnats I referred to while swallowing the behavioral camels of hatred, greed and blatant materialism, older evangelicals have presented to the world a hollow travesty of the gospel. We have made the commands of God to stink because we used them selectively to justify our way of life. We left large segments of Scripture unexpounded —we, too, loved darkness (Jn. 3:19)—until it became clear to everyone around us that if the ethic we stood for was a biblical one, then a biblical ethic was inadequate. Situational ethics represents a crude attempt to remedy the glaring areas in the negative ethic we preached. For we did not preach a biblical ethic at all.

Scriptural Freedom and Sex

We have failed not only in our emphasis, which was a neurotic obsession rather than a sign of holiness, but in our exegesis. The Scripture gives reasons for its proscription of premarital and extramarital sex. "Thou shalt not!" is not the heart, and certainly not the purpose, of God's command. God has no need to explain his edicts, yet in this case he chose to do so.

Long before Paul gets to our favorite part of I Corinthians 6 (the part where he deplores the incongruity of our being a temple of the Spirit and united to a harlot), he discusses the issue of freedom.

"I am free to do anything," you say. Yes, but not every-thing is for my good. No doubt I am free to do anything, but I for one will not let anything make free with me. "Food is for the belly and the belly for food," you say. True; and one day God will put an end to both. *But it is not true that the body is for lust; it is for the Lord.* (1 Cor. 6:12-14, NEB, my emphasis)

"I am free to do anything." Hurrah for freedom! What a great thing it is! Freedom is what we most need, freedom from our hypocritical inhibitions.

But what is freedom?

Paul defines it in terms of purpose, of what something is designed or made for. ("The body is not for fornication.") We live in a world where everything has a design and a func-tion. You don't set a fish free from the ocean (poor fish! so confined and restricted!) or birds from the necessity of flight. Birds were designed to fly and fish to swim. They are freest when they are doing what they were designed to do. In the same way your body was not designed for premarital sex and will never be truly free when you engage in it.

But freedom is also an experience. We cannot know whether fish *feel* free in the ocean or birds in the air. From outside them, by observing them, we could make an equally good case for their being totally enslaved in the sense that they are slaves of their instincts and environment. Fish cannot live in the air or birds in the ocean.

The experience of freedom has to do with being loved and loving. God designed you because he loved you. His purposes for you are an expression of his love to you. And as you re-spond in love to his commands (about sex or anything else) you are set free, free to be and to do what both you and God want. The more completely you are enslaved in love to his blessed will, the freer you will discover yourself to be. No one who has ever tasted the freedom of being the slave of Christ will doubt the breathtaking sense of set-freeness that charac-terizes it.

The Dead Issue of Petting

How does all this work out in relation to premarital sex? How does it work out with couples who pet? What happens?

Why, the more they pet the less they talk. And the less they talk the more they pet. Whenever they are together they wish they could be alone. When they are alone, their eyes glaze over as they grope past buttons to flesh. Freedom?

What kind of an approach to life commitment is that? Though sexuality is designed to facilitate freedom in communication, paradoxically it hinders communication when it is abused. We saw in an earlier chapter how masturbation defeats the instinct it gratifies. The same is true of petting.

It seems only yesterday when the gravest topic in Christian youth magazines had to do with adolescent petting. How far to go? Should one hold hands on a date? Kiss? Embrace? Touch? Fondle?

In retrospect it seems quaint. The attempt to control sexual standards by discouraging petting has been as effective as a paper fence in a flood. Young people all over the world are losing their freedom in a battle against enslavement to lust. True sexual freedom is being eroded and destroyed.

I grant that sexual practices of Christian young people lag behind those of their non-Christian counterparts in "freedom." But it is also true that petting has been superseded even in evangelical circles by the issue of premarital sexual intercourse.

In fact the issue has always been that. How does one distinguish between petting and intercourse? Once you try to map out morality in terms of anatomy and physiology, you wind up with an ethical labyrinth from which there is no exit.

Take the example of a kiss. Can anyone take seriously a Roman Catholic writer who distinguished innocent kisses, venial sin kisses and mortal sin kisses by the number of seconds the lips touched? It is true that the further you proceed with physical contact the nearer you come to coitus. But defining coitus in terms of penetration and orgasm has as much moral significance and as much logical difficulty as trying to define a beard by the number of hairs on a chin.

I know that experts used to distinguish light from heavy petting, and heavy petting from intercourse, but is there any moral difference between two naked people in bed petting to orgasm and another two having intercourse? Is the one act a fraction of an ounce less sinful than the other?

Is it perhaps more righteous to pet with clothes on? If so, which is worse, to pet with clothes off or to have intercourse with clothes on?

You may accuse me of being crude. Far from it. If we pursue the argument far enough we will see that an approach to the morality of premarital sex which is based on details of behavior (kissing, dressing or undressing, touching, holding, looking) and of parts of the body (fingers, hair, arms, breasts, lips, genitalia) can only satisfy a pharisee. A look can be as sensual as a touch, and a finger brushed lightly over a cheek as erotic as a penetration.

There are no moral mileposts on the slippery slope down to detumescence. If you scramble off it before getting there you may be proving something (likely your cowardice) but certainly not your virtue.

Premarital petting and premarital intercourse are not two issues but one. They sound like separate issues. They look like separate issues. As little as ten years ago most Christian couples thought of premarital intercourse as out of the question. But in the seventies the ethical issues have become fuzzier through situational thinking, and the taboo has been weakened because we have all become so used to sexual sin.

Where on the long road from caressing to conceiving is a Christian supposed to stop? One "Christian" magazine I came across some years ago firmly recommended contraception, arguing that while the sexual relationship could be "very meaningful," pregnancy in such circumstances was "irresponsible." Many young people today, whether Christian or non-Christian, would rightly reject such thinking as hypocritical.

Several paragraphs back I declared that there were no moral milestones along the road. If I am right, if it is also true that a touch is no different from a penetration and if premarital sexual intercourse is wrong, then the whole bag of tricks is wrong.

How should couples view the time of their engagement? Should they not use it to explore each other's hearts and minds rather than each other's bodies?

How clearly have they discussed their marriage goals? How explicit have they been in expressing what each expects of the other in marriage in duties and interests shared or divided, finances, Christian behavior in the home, the training of children? These are not issues decided by ticking off squares on a computer card. How easily can the couple talk about their deepest emotions? Their likes and dislikes?

What have been termed "necking" and "petting" constitute what sexologists call foreplay. Kissing, touching, caressing prepare the bodies of the participants for physical intercourse. They are a part of a whole. Sexual intercourse does not begin when a penis penetrates a vagina (husbands who think it does have a lot to learn) but when people in love allow their fingers to interlock or when a hand tenderly strokes a lock of hair. If premarital intercourse is sinful, so are necking and petting. So also is a lustful look. Petting is a dead issue.

To take the position I have taken means that the only real issue we must face is the legitimacy of premarital sexual relations. The problem is as old as humanity, and societies in different ages and places have all had to grapple with this same question.

In the recent past no evangelical Christians have questioned the wrongness of premarital sex. But in the seventies the older generation feels bewildered and helpless as it watches the sexual revolution taking place. Some of my young friends have told me that "nearly all" Christian couples now go to bed before they go to the altar. I think they are exaggerating. Some, it is true, live together openly. Others indulge in cozy weekends. An unknown number are sneaky.

But just as disturbing as their behavior is its casual justification. "Of course it's all right," is the attitude of some. "It
isn't really that important." "It's healthy." "It's the natural
thing to do." "It's one's motivation that matters." "We're
not promiscuous. We're just as faithful as married people.
And we are faithful because we love each other, not because of
what society thinks."

Parents have always known that one thing leads to another.
Parental anxiety about children's sexual behavior has been
mounting over the past decade. It is a concern that has irri-
tated the younger couples, at times driving them further in
the direction of sexual relations. Both sides can be to blame, a
fact that everyone involved discovers when pregnancy forces
them all to face reality. In a healthy family, at such a time, parents lay aside their shame and children lay aside their defiance
as both realize their mutual need and their mutual depend-
ence.

The parents' failure as well as their source of pain has been
their pride in their children. Believing they wish to protect
their children "for their (the children's) own happiness," they
have really been equally concerned with scandal.

What mother enjoys facing the prayer circle knowing every
woman there is aware of her daughter's pregnancy? What
father is not humbled before his peers when that same
daughter comes back from college silently proclaiming her
nonvirginity with every step she takes?

In some dim way parents may sense their guilt and failure.
They respond to it differently. Some send their daughters on
a long vacation. Others make hurried marriage preparations.
Still others, respecting their children's need and right to make
certain choices themselves, hide their pain and make themselves available to meet their children's needs. As for the children, awareness of what they have done to others can lead to
a greater sense of responsibility. It is one thing to scorn the
petty rigidity and pride of one's parents or to protest one's

right to make his own decisions. It is quite another to observe the pain and humiliation of the parents whose views are held in contempt and to contemplate one's responsibility to a life to be.

Strange that it should take a pregnancy to shake us all free of our vanity. Conception out of wedlock seems to be the crime. With good reason it was called "getting caught" by a previous generation.

The Case for Premarital Sex
Why should there be any question in the minds of evangelicals about premarital sex? Are we not characterized by our adherence to Scripture? Let us again remind ourselves of St. Paul's attitude. "Fornication and indecency of any kind ... must not be so much as mentioned among you, as befits the people of God" (Eph. 5:3, NEB). What could be clearer?

In the past an appeal to Scripture was enough. Why is it so no longer? For it is impossible to examine the issue of premarital sex without discovering that many of its proponents are not prepared to accept New Testament teaching, evangelical moorings notwithstanding.

Already we have discussed the biblical underpinnings of the rules about sex. Our bodies were designed for freedom. Freedom can be found in sex or in any other area only when we fulfill the purpose of our creation.

If you talk to many younger folk from evangelical homes, however, you may hear them protesting the rigidity of the rules. You slowly become aware of a ground swell of feeling that rejects the sexual standards of the church (scriptural or not) because they are hypocritical, prejudice-bound and irrelevant. How has the change come about?

The remarks I have been quoting have the ring of the so-called new morality and of situational ethics. A situational ethic denies that morality can be codified. Right or wrong must be defined by the elements of the situation in which I find myself. The motive is more important than the act, why I do something rather than what it is I do. Fornication under certain circumstances is right. Love is the basic principle in a truly Christian ethic for love is the fulfilling of the law.

I may be wrong, but I do not believe that situation ethics is responsible for the confused justification of contemporary sexual standards or the consequent rejection of certain specific parts of Scripture. The boot is on the other foot. While it is true that wrong belief can produce wrong actions, it is even more true that our desire to do wrong makes us seize on any ethical system which justifies us. *We distort Scripture because we do not like what it says and not because we have found a superior ethic.* "Men loved darkness rather than light, because their deeds were evil" (Jn. 3:19). In any case I am very suspicious of the "love" that is used to defy a scriptural principle.

Love is the fulfilling of the law. It truly sums up biblical morality. But the love that fulfills the law is not the glazed, heavy-breathed stirring in the groins that clouds your judgment and seduces your will as you copulate. It is not the love that you *make*. Premarital sexual excitement too often becomes all-important, as many unmarried people have discovered. It blocks the very communication it is designed to promote.

Love is more than pity, greater than compassion, deeper than understanding and more positive than self-denial. It is the agape love of 1 Corinthians 13, the love that originates in the heart of God, the love that cannot stop when the love object ceases to please.

Such a love explains the moral law rather then abolishes it. To seize a cliché from the enemy, the commands of Scripture become "meaningful" as they are illuminated by agape. By love's light we see no irrelevancies in the biblical proscription of premarital or extramarital sex. They are utterly germane to the modern situation.

I do not defend the laws of Scripture. They need no defense. They exist. That is enough. I seek only to explain why they begin to seem irrelevant to a generation already confused and bewildered by social change. Yet we must look at more of the arguments used to justify a less stringent morality.

Playboy Sex

Playboy magazine represents a kind of philosophical approach to sexual pleasure. Playboy is more than pornography. In it Hugh Heffner tries very seriously to teach a way of life. His outlook bases itself, among other things, on the premise that pleasure needs no justification. Enjoyment is good so let us get rid of our hang-ups and accept it.

I hardly need to discuss a Playboy approach to sex. Its view of woman is selfish and male-oriented, and its concept of pleasure unrealistic.

Pleasure is as difficult to pursue as the end of a rainbow. Look for pleasure and you never find it. Whenever you try to seize it by the tail, it eludes you.

Had pleasure been as easy to find as it is to pursue, the school of Epicurean philosophy would never have gotten off the ground. Greeks of years gone by found that the problem of pleasure was a deep and serious one and that it became the more insoluble the more serious the pursuit of pleasure became.

For pleasure is a by-product, a side effect. It takes us by surprise when we are looking for something else.

I tried the broken cisterns, Lord,
But, ah! the waters failed.
E'en as I stooped to drink they fled,
And mocked me as I wailed.

Seek God and you find, among other things, piercing pleasure. Seek pleasure and in the long run you find boredom, disillusionment and enslavement. So even if *Playboy* were right in saying that it is good to pursue pleasure, the pursuit would lead to flatness, disappointment and enslavement.

"But It Feels So Right!"

Some, however, throw philosophy to the winds. "It *feels* so

58

right, so healthy," says the nineteen-year-old girl whose blonde hair softly caresses her slim shoulders. "How can it be wrong when I'm just glad to give Joe what he wants when it feels so wholesome."

Yes, dear heart, and the thing itself *is* wholesome. (Perhaps you didn't expect me to say that?) It's not copulation that is bad but the way you use it. Good food is wholesome. To have a steak dinner, when it might have been better to complete an assignment, can be justified in exactly the same way. When you sigh contentedly as you move from the steak house back to the car you can say with profound conviction: "Thank you, honey. That was just great. We needed that. I'm sure it was right to put off the assignment."

And you may be right or wrong. But one thing is certain: Eating steak, in itself, is perfectly wholesome. It is not immoral, unclean or dirty. What makes it right or wrong has to do with the circumstances under which you ate it. Your positive feelings are unreliable guides especially where uncompleted assignments are involved, just as they are in the case of premarital sex. A feeling of rightness proves nothing except to the person who wants it to.

Sex and Mental Health
But what about sex and mental health?

Books without number have been telling us that from the point of view of mental health, premarital and extramarital sex can have value.

The most strident advocate of sexual expression and mental health was the late psychoanalyst Wilhelm Reich, a man whose books were for a time suppressed. In his most famous book, *Character Analysis*[2], he argues the central importance of achieving orgasms of sufficient quantity and qualitative intensity if one is to become a mature and well-rounded person. An orgasm a day will keep the doctor away, so to speak. For the orgasm is the "nexus where soul and body meet" and around which character is formed. Nonsense—but nonsense which was greeted with the reverence devoted to prophetic utterances by a growing body of Reich's admirers.

More moderate psychological and psychiatric theory has to do with the unhealthy repressing of bodily instincts. Once again I must insist that supression and repression are not the same thing.

Repression of sex urges is unhealthy. It is unhealthy because it is born of fear and guilt. When fear and guilt drive my sexual urges underground, I do indeed need to be set free. Buried fear lays foundation for an unhealthy sexual life.

Suppression, on the other hand, is not only healthy but also necessary for my emotional development. My sex desires are a God-given part of me. I do not need to be ashamed of them, guilty about them or afraid of them. But there are times when I must say to them, as I say to my dog, "Lie down now! Some other time, but not now!" Like my dog they may not want to obey. But they must be trained, and I must be the master.

You see, I am not repressing my dog but suppressing him when I say, "Lie down!" I don't feel ashamed of him when visitors come. If I felt guilty or ashamed, I would hide him in the basement, and I would feel very bothered about the howls and mess that would result. On the contrary I am proud of him. But I must teach him his place. Not to do so would result in unhappiness for him, for me and for my guests. I would lose friends. They would resent being jumped on, pawed, scratched and licked. My hound in addition would be bewildered and hurt by a rejection he could not possibly comprehend.

Sexual drives (like pet police dogs) need to be suppressed and trained for their real place in our lives if we are to experience healthy development and not become sexual slobs.

The Pill
I must raise one more point before we discuss how to solve premarital entanglements. Some sociologists tell us that the pill has created the sexual revolution.

Has it?

Was there no premarital sex in Rome? In Regency London? In Paris? In most rural areas in Europe among peasant classes? Did such sex ever *only* involve young men and houses of prostitution? The pill has made things easier than they used to be for girls to avoid pregnancy but no essential change has taken place.

Sex used to be a little riskier, but pregnancy could always be avoided by people who wanted to. And what has avoiding pregnancy to do with the rightness or wrongness of premarital sex? The much touted pill is another of man's technical triumphs over nature making it more possible for us to avoid the consequences but not one whit better to do so.

Facing the Practical Problems

Let me begin by summarizing the Bible's teaching on the wrongness of fornication. Let me summarize how distorted teaching has undermined the crumbling walls of morality.

We have distorted the Scriptures by emphasizing externals more than Scripture does (smoking, dancing, drinking, promiscuity and so on) and by thus *presenting holiness in negative terms*. We have failed to stress the nature of and the reason for positive holiness of life. Holiness itself has become either a form of legalism (by which we contribute to the cost of our salvation) or a sort of pseudopsychological lift by which we will be more "greatly used" or have a "fuller life." The principle reason for holiness as commanded in Scripture is "You shall be holy; for I the LORD your God am holy" (Lev. 19:2).

Sensing the hollowness of our lopsided Bible preaching, young and old alike have been unprepared for the dual onslaught of increasing sexual stimulation and the subtleties of new sexual philosophies. Something had to fill the gap and something had to give.

Fornication is wrong because it defeats God's purpose for your sexuality. It replaces freedom with bondage and closes the door to the deepest intimacies of all. Let me spell this out.

Your body does not belong to you but to God whether you call yourself a Christian or not.

Your sexuality likewise is not yours but his.

Far from being mean and restrictive about sex God wants you to experience the fullest possible enjoyment of it consistent with your happiness. He wants to make you sexually free.

You can only *enjoy* sex *in freedom.* "The body is not meant for immorality, but for the Lord" (1 Cor. 6:13). In other words the purpose of your sexuality was that you might know intimate love (which is wider and deeper than physical sex) within the secure and growing framework of marriage. Any other use of it will not free you but enslave you. You have only two options: to be free within God's purposes for you or to be a slave to sex, to yourself and to others outside of his purposes (1 Cor. 6:12). If my statement makes you feel trapped, then you have never known what real freedom feels like.

When you indulge in premarital sex, you do something which is fundamentally against nature and against the instincts God placed within you. You sin against your own body, that is, you do something detrimental to the very purpose of its creation (1 Cor. 6:18).

But what if you are already having premarital sex or if you are counseling someone else who is? What should you do in a situation like this?

Breaking Off Sexual Relationships
It is easier when both of you decide to break off. It is roughest when only one of you is convinced.

Is your relationship one of love? Are you thinking seriously of marriage? or just hoping? Is there a possibility that he or she will break off the relationship altogether if you quit having sex? If the last question hits home, you may have been selling your birthright for a mess of pottage.

There is only one way to find out. Tell your lover. Face to face. But not in your "special place."

You may need the prayer support of a neutral friend you can trust. You will have to be absolutely certain in your mind. Perhaps you feel you cannot face the pain of a possible breakup. Well you can. On the other hand you may face a joyous surprise when you find the one whose love you doubted, loves and respects you more than you thought. It could go either way.

Therefore the decision (about breaking off sexual relations whatever the consequences) has to be made *before* you discuss it. It has to be made firmly and, as far as lies in you, unambivalently. The only discussion has to do not with *whether* or even with *when* but with *how*.

How in the future are you going to react to a squeeze? to a kiss? Ought you still to hold hands?

No one can decide these things for you. The only criterion to guide you will be what kisses, squeezes and holding hands do for either or both of you. Do they turn you on sexually? Do they make it harder to communicate at levels you ought to be communicating? Do they lower your resistance to old patterns of interaction? An affectionate caress becomes sex play the moment it begins to pull your thoughts from what you should be sharing to what you should not. The correct Scripture will at that point be, "Flee temptation" (1 Tim. 6:9-11).

Supposing when you level with your lover, the worst thing happens. Supposing he or she reacts angrily, resentfully, accusingly? Supposing it means total rejection?

I can only say that the God who wants you to be free is also compassionate. "As a Father pities his children, so the LORD pities those who fear him. For he knows our frame; he remembers that we are dust." (Ps. 103:13-14). His only Son, who loved you and died for you, tells you that "even the hairs of your head are all numbered" (Mt. 10:30).

It is inevitable that a breakup will leave a wound, perhaps a deep one, that will take time to heal. But if you let the Healer lay his hand on it, the wound will heal more gently, more rapidly, more sweetly. You may weep, but God will store up your tears in a bottle (Ps. 56:8), so precious are they to him. And through the whole process you will find richer companionship in him while he may at the same time begin to lay the foundations for a deeper companionship with your future husband or wife.

Marriage in the Sight of God?
Is premarital sex "marriage in the sight of God"? No: Most certainly not.

Marriage, to be marriage must be entered into *as marriage* by both partners. It has been thus throughout history. In Genesis men "took" women "in marriage." The contract was carried out in the presence of witnesses and in accordance with local customs. (Scripture never speaks of marriage as a sacrament so that the heathen marriage, a non-Christian marriage, and a marriage between Christians in a church building are all equally binding and permanent in the sight of God. Christians are not *more* married than heathens. Marriage has, like the sun and rain, been given by God to all men equally.)

Fornication is sin. Marriage (in and of itself) is holy. Whence then the idea that when single people copulate (that is, commit sin), they are "married in the sight of God" (that is, entering a holy estate)? Of course what the phrase means to imply is that if you copulate you ought to marry the person you have sex with. Dilemma: Which one? The first one? ("But I wasn't the first one for *him*. And *he* wasn't the first one for her." Confusion . . .)

Behind the mistaken notion that premarital sex demands that the partners marry is a wrongly understood biblical command. Twice in the Old Testament the command is given to a man who seduces a virgin to marry her and also to pay her dowry price. (Ex. 22:16-17; Deut. 22:28-29). If a man and an unbetrothed girl were caught having intercourse, the man was assumed to be to blame.

It is interesting that in Deuteronomy the being found is specifically mentioned. Not that getting caught is the crime or that seduction in secret is less immoral. The whole point (compare the two accounts) is that the girl in both cases is publicly compromised. Her chances of a respectable marriage are reduced and her dowry price falls. Two people, according to local customs, have thus been wronged—the seduced girl and her father. The account in Exodus also makes it clear that the marriage is not absolutely essential. What is essential is that the dowry price be paid by the offending Don Juan.

Now whatever problems my interpretation raises (and it does raise interesting points), one thing is quite clear. Sexual relations do not constitute marriage in the sight of God or anyone else. They may or may not be grounds for forcing a man to get married (depending on what his prospective father-in-law thinks of him). But because of local customs and in the light of those customs, the law institutes a fair deal for father and daughter. And whenever a man seduced an unattached girl, this was the sort of risk he ran.

Such local traditions no longer exist. The biblical principle involved still does. It teaches us that law should protect the rights of the sexually wronged. This and no more.

But suppose I feel I ought to marry her or him? If it was wrong for me to have sex with her, don't I owe her something?

Yes, you do. You owe her an apology. Nothing more? Yes, much more. You owe it to her to quit fooling with her or him and not to make it any more difficult than you already have. And you owe it to consider carefully before God what the future of your relationship ought to be. You cannot go on as you are at present. So how will you go on?

I will talk more about marriage in relation to sin in the next section. For the time being you should remember three things. First, two people have to be willing to marry before a marriage can take place. The other partner may not want to marry. Any armtwisting based on working on someone's guilt feelings is wrong and can be a highway to a wrecked marriage. Do not force someone to marry you by making him feel guilty. (Do not, if you are a parent, force your child or anyone else's to marry by telling them they ought to.) Do not let anyone make you feel you have sinned and therefore you ought to marry. Your feelings of guilt are not a good basis for marriage. They must be dealt with before marriage and not atoned for by marriage. Marriage may in fact add to the wrong you are doing by plunging two people who should never be married into a life of conjugal hell.

Second, if you are feeling guilty, recognize where your guilt feelings come from. If they come because God's Holy Spirit is convicting you of sins committed, then confess your sin to him. If you cannot remember all the details of your sin, no matter. God is not a celestial voyeur. It is your attitude of repentance and faith that matters. Firmly and boldly and by faith you must go into the holiest of all where you will find an open and loving welcome if you go sprinkled by blood.

But recognize that not all guilt feeling arises from true guilt. The Holy Spirit can convict, but Satan can also accuse. In fact day and night every time you kneel in God's presence to pray he does so (Rev. 12:10). You must not let him impede your access to the holiest place of all. Tell him he has no business demanding that you show your admission ticket to the inner sanctum. He belongs to the wrong outfit. God accepts you because of his Son's death. It does not matter what people think, even your lover. (Is he still hurt in spite of your having done all you can to amend matters?) God's acceptance and forgiveness are based on none of these things. They are not based on your sincerity and genuineness of your spiritual endeavors, but ever, only and always on the merits of Christ. God invites you to him because his Son died for you. Christ's death, and that alone, atones for all your guilt.

Third, if you feel that marriage in the future is what you should consider (not based on false feelings of guilt), go to an experienced person whose spiritual insight you can trust. Go to one who will let you talk. And when he comments, listen. You don't have to accept his advice, but ponder it well.

"Honey, I Think I'm Pregnant."

I mentioned earlier that it takes a pregnancy to shake some of us loose from our phoney attitudes. Unfortunately it also takes a pregnancy to bring out the worst in lovers, their friends and their parents.

Angie and Tom in their panic asked, "How can we get an abortion?" And when they told their parents, Angie's mother as well as Angie, the mother-to-be, both wanted it.

Sometimes the young mother-to-be may have mixed feelings and, frequently, an ardent desire to keep her baby. Inside her body and nervous system God's delicate mechanisms are preparing every part of her physically and emotionally to care for a new life. It is not surprising then that fifteen-year-old girls angrily reject the urgings of older people to "have an abortion." The surprising thing is that not all of them feel the same way.

Abortions may be legal or illegal. In the United States, in Britain, in various European countries, in Japan and in Canada they can be carried out legally and in some of these countries simply on the demand of the pregnant woman or girl. You may walk into a clinic pregnant, be examined, slated for a simple removal of the pregnancy (if it is an early one) and after a varying number of hours, walk home.

Few Christians are happy about abortion on demand. Many are not happy about abortion at all, even when carried out by conscientious physicians for medical or psychiatric reasons.

Usually if you want an abortion, you check with your family physician. If he feels there may be medical grounds for one (that is, if he feels that the pregnancy will jeopardize your physical or emotional health), he will refer you to two other physicians, usually specialists. One will usually be a gynecologist and the other a psychiatrist. Both of these will in turn submit reports on you to a hospital abortion board.

The red tape is a way (which never delays abortions, for every day makes an abortion less safe) of making sure things are not done sneakily. Records are kept. As far as those most expert in health are concerned, a careful assessment is made to predict whether a pregnancy would be harmful in any way to mother or child or whether the abortion is needed for the girl's well-being.

But how often can the experts tell? Sometimes they can't. At other times they are guessing. Sometimes they are swayed, consciously or unconsciously, by their own religious and political views. If all the doctors involved are Jews, you are more likely to get an abortion than if they are all Catholics. For moral values enter in whether we choose to let them or not.

I am not qualified to discuss the morality of medical abortions. I believe that under certain circumstances an abortion may constitute the lesser of two evils (the evil of allowing potential life to come into being as a true life only to destroy the health or even the life of the mother or the evil of destroying the potential life). I would like to say more about it, but people wiser than I have already said much more than I could say and have said it better.

One thing I will say about abortion. I see nothing whatever to justify abortion as an easy way of dodging embarrassment and shame. If all that is at stake is your pride or your reputation, then you may be destroying more than a potential life. You will be destroying your integrity, be you parent advising it or girl accepting it.

If you do not destroy the pregnancy, then you let it continue. The question that then arises is, What do you do about the baby? Seventeen-year-old Cheryl's father had died two years before Cheryl's baby (sired by a long-haired, unemployed boy friend) would be due. She was halfway through eleventh grade and three months pregnant. Cheryl's own mother had the backbone of a jellyfish. Her sole contribution to family discussions on the pregnancy was to cry and to wish that her dear Harry had never died for "then all this would never have happened." But Cheryl had aunts who were not jellyfish and who whisked Cheryl off from Saskatoon, where she lived, to stay with relatives in Vancouver.

Cheryl had neutral feelings about her boy friend but desperately wanted to keep her baby. ("It's got at least a part of my dad in it, and he's the only person I ever really loved.") A social worker from Welfare talked to Cheryl in Vancouver. Cheryl slowly came to see some of the very real problems that would face a girl of eighteen (her age when the baby was due) with an uncompleted education if she were to try to bring up a child in the teeth of powerful family opposition. (Remember Cheryl's mother didn't really count.) Cheryl was still dazed when, the day after the baby was born, she signed away all her claims on the baby's future life on adoption papers the social worker had filled out for her. She had never seen her baby and she never would.

"It's much better that way," said the aunt with the backbone. Many people would nod in agreement.

During the next eighteen months Cheryl made four suicide attempts, two of them serious ones. She is strongly suicidal at the date of writing, but she is not mentally ill unless we consider the suicide drive itself a form of mental illness. She is under psychiatric care trying to come to terms with who she is and what she did when she gave her baby away.

I could fill a book with stories of what has happened to illegitimate babies I have known or known about and of all the people involved with their fates. But from Cheryl's story you can see that the problem was not just Cheryl's problem. Her family may have made the wrong decision, but they had to make some decision. So did her boy friend. Had Cheryl kept the baby, someone would have had to care for it had she (as she wished to) continued her education. High schools do not budget for day care centers for their students' babies.

The problems of the other family members become all the more acute the younger the girl is and the less the prospective father is in a position to support the baby. Fourteen-year-old Janet's mother struggled with her conscience for weeks before deciding against abortion of Janet's illegitimate pregnancy. Janet was glad. She did not want to marry her sixteen-year-old drop-out boy friend. ("I like him, but he's spaced out on drugs most of the time.") What she wanted to do was skip a year of school, have her baby and bring it up at home, then complete her education. Her father threatened to throw her out of the house.

Her cultured (and very open) Catholic mother wept in my office. It was not the problem of her angry husband that bothered her. "Janet won't consider letting the baby be adopted," she said. "The nuns have talked to her and so has a social worker who specializes in these problems. I didn't want more babies. Even though we're Catholics my husband and I deliberately stopped at three. Janet is our youngest. The other two are boys. I know I shouldn't feel this way about it, but whatever Janet says, I know *I'm* going to be the real mother of that baby, not Janet. And I feel wicked for resenting it."

I felt a lot of respect for that woman. She at least had the courage to face her true feelings.

To cut the discussion down a little, you may be beginning to see that the main alternatives facing families with illegitimate pregnancies are the following: (1) "Shotgun marriages," (that is, "We-had-to-get-married" marriages); (2) abortion (with or without "hushing up"); (3) adopting out (with or without "hushing up"); and (4) the incorporation of the illegitimate baby, somehow, into the larger family unit.

These are not, as some of my discussion must have made clear, mutually exclusive alternatives. Moreover in this book I cannot discuss them in detail. What I propose to do is to make brief comments on the first and last possibilities before concluding this chapter.

Shotgun Marriages

Let me remind you of the position I have already adopted, namely that there is no scriptural justification for saying that fornication—even fornication issuing in pregnancy—must be "made right" by marriage.

If Joe feels he should "do right by" Mary, let him by all

means own up to being the father and go on record on the birth certificate as being so. But let both Joe and Mary, as well as their parents, be slow about opting for marriage.

It could be the right thing. Or it could be disastrous.

Young people considering marriage under these circumstances find it hard to believe that things could go wrong. But they do. They go wrong because of the basis of the marriage. Any marriage can go wrong, but the marriages we are talking about already have the odds loaded against them.

I am speaking not of engaged girls who get pregnant but more particularly of those who become pregnant before they had made any public commitment to marry (that is, before the couple was officially engaged). Against such a marriage the odds are more than usually loaded. Why?

Whenever, years later, anything goes wrong, the beginning of the marriage is never forgotten by either partner. When doubts arise in Mary's mind about Joe's love, she will find herself saying one day, "He married me because he had to, and now he's regretting it. Perhaps he didn't really love me, even when we married." I hear such words spoken in my office.

Unfortunately she may be right. For when stresses arise, Joe may feel trapped, trapped in a marriage by a false sense of obligation. "After all," he may find himself saying, "she was at least as much to blame for what happened as I." (These words, too, get expressed in my office.)

Or the resentment may never even reach a conscious level in either of them but fester, deep below the surface, and bubble up in ways that neither partner can understand.

Please be clear as to what I am arguing. I am not arguing that such a marriage should be dissolved. The only point I am making here is that everyone involved should think hard *before the marriage takes place.*

In subtle and unconscious ways, too, the attitudes of both parents to the first child may differ from their attitudes to subsequent children. Guilt feelings, unconscious resentments about what the pregnancy led to, like the part of the iceberg

71

below the surface of the water, affect the relationship between the first child and his parents. And it may take months or years before any of them have the insight to realize what is going on.

But lest I drive to despair some who have already married "because they had to," I must also say that such problems are neither inevitable nor insoluble. God does have answers for them. If both of you are prepared to face what has been going on in your heart, to discuss with each other the fears and resentments that trouble you, to deal before God with your inner resentments, then the very weak points of your marriage can become its greatest strengths. But you must face them, not brush them under the carpet.

Three Factions and One Family

Dan and Emily, a happily married couple in their mid-forties, were pastoring a fundamentalist church in a northern U.S. city. They had four children (two married boys and two girls still in high school). Tragedy struck when their youngest daughter, Nanette, became pregnant by George, son of the chairman of the church board who was a prominent and wealthy businessman.

George (nineteen, in junior college and active in Christian work) said, "I don't dare tell the old man. He'll kill me." Neither he nor Nanette had considered marriage. Though George was willing to marry Nanette, Nanette was less sure. Against George's anxious urging, Nanette told her mother, "I thought I loved him and that I wasn't doing wrong," she wept a little. "Now I'm not sure about anything."

Pastor Dan and his wife very soon met with George's parents and the young couple to talk the matter over. What was said and who said what is not really clear. Within a week a dozen versions of the affair were secretly delighting the gossip circles in the congregation and adding to the distress of the two families involved.

Several points of view emerged and were taken up by different church factions. First, there were those who said that a man whose daughter plays around with sex is not fit to be a pastor. His children should be an example. How can we expect our young people . . . etc., etc.? (Nanette spent two nights crying sleeplessly over that one.) Then there was the "They ought to get married" faction who generally seemed to feel that "least said, sooner mended."

Another faction was the 1 Corinthians 5 faction. Sin had been committed; therefore public confession had to be made. But (and it was a big and serious but) how did we know the young couple had repented of their sin? Supposing they were still having sex in secret? When they really repented, let them marry, be put out of the church for a short period of discipline, and then be brought back into fellowship.

Some people said that George's father ought to resign from the board, but George's father seemed unaware of the feeling. Few people made unpleasant suggestions to George's father about anything.

The details of all that followed are painful and unnecessary for us to go into. The friendship of George's and Nanette's parents came to an end. No marriage took place. George was the only one who favored it and George's will was not a match for his father's. In any case Nanette was still uncertain about marriage. "If he still wants to marry me two years from now and if I can be sure by that time that I love him enough to marry him, then I will but not now."

Pastor Dan, Emily and their two daughters had to leave the church (morning congregation 1,200; membership 760) and eventually, after a period of unemployment, were called to a country Methodist church (independent) to whom they told the whole story. Nanette is currently in eleventh grade and Jonni, her baby boy, is seven months old. Emily and Nanette share the care of him—Emily's share being the larger just now. It is agreed among them all that Jonni will call Nanette "mommy" and Emily will be called "grammy". No secret will be made about his paternity and every effort will be made to prepare him for the burden of the social stigma of his illegitimacy.

The family is absolutely united on the course of action they have adopted. There have been (and still are) disagreements about how practical duties (like diaper washing) are to be shared, and there are still occasional bouts of uncertainty and weeping. But surprisingly enough the family knows more contentment and joy than they have known for years. Each member faced personal crises concerning his or her goals in life, sense of values and relationship with God. It is evident that the presence of God is in their home and the hand of God on their ministry.

I cannot possibly enter into a discussion of all the enormous questions that Nanette's story opens up for us. I write about it for a reason that is close to my heart and that encourages me to write about sexual sin. Like all sin, it can, when it comes to light bring unspeakable pain for many people. But it has the same potential for joy and growth as it has for pain. Everything depends on how each person involved responds to the situation.

In Nanette's case her sin opened doors of fire not only to herself but to other members of her family, doors through which they passed into a quality of fellowship with God they had never known before. "It took a minor earthquake to make me see how shallow my Christian service was," Pastor Dan says. The family is poorer financially and in prestige but much richer in love, joy and fellowship.

It is as I look at Pastor Dan's family that I begin to see how the cross of Christ, rightly understood, is indeed a gateway to glory.

5
THE
SCARLET
LETTER

Augustine wrote, "For I was loved myself, and I reached the point where we met together to enjoy our love, and there I was fettered happily in bonds of misery so that I might be beaten with red-hot iron—the rods of jealousy and suspicions, and fears and angers and quarrels."[1]

Foolishly I once tried to classify people who had extramarital affairs much as ornithologists classify birds. But I gave up the attempt. Adulterers cannot be classified. They may be old, young; cultured, crude; lusty, refined; selfish, generous; kindly, cruel, and even, if we use the term with the slightest degree of flexibility, spiritual or carnal. If we must make distinctions, we must not make them in people but in the attitudes people adopt to what they do.

Any married person can commit adultery. The conscience-lashed Puritan preacher of Hawthorne's *The Scarlet Letter* is as likely a candidate as a Casanova or a Don Juan. A Jew, a Catholic, a Quaker and a Pentecostal can all be committers of adultery; a business convention and a religious revival can both be occasions for it while cars, doctors' offices, homes and church offices are all possible places for the practice of it.

You cannot distinguish adulterers by class, color or creed but by their attitudes to their behavior. Some slowly strangle their consciences and let their self-indulgence grow like fungus. Some laugh and seem to have no conscience. Others are cowardly but go on in adultery because they cringe timidly at the thought of offending their lovers. These are the most miserably enslaved.

God touches some; and because they feel his touch, they repent and make what amends they can. Yet others, and when I think of these anger burns in me, proclaim that sin is virtue, that adultery is only a dirty word to besmirch something noble. Narrow religious hypocrites have made adultery *seem* unclean.

When such ideas fall on my ears from the lips of educated people with a Christian background, my heart beats and my hands tremble.

The New Adulterers and Sexspeak

I call such people The New Adulterers even though their philosophy is really as ancient as the history of philosophy itself. A number of books have recently been published on the alternatives to marriage expressing the view of The New Adulterers.[2]

Margaret Mead has for years suggested that we accept the alternative of "serial monogomy." And now, with equal seriousness, Alvin Toffler proposes in his best seller, *Future Shock,* that mobile executives in large corporations may in the future stop moving their families with them when promotion demands a cross-country switch. Family units and homes should remain as "plug in" facilities for executives on the move. Instead of finding him a suitable house, the company should find him a suitably matched house-family-unit facility, with similar wife and children to the old unit he just unplugged from.

The New Adulterers bother me for two reasons. To begin with they contemptuously toss the ancient rules into the garbage can. Their arrogance offends me. What matter that people have for centuries tested and proved their worth! Rules that may have been relevant in earlier, less complex cultures are inappropriate in our sophisticated age. They will coolly tell me, "Yes, we did go to bed together. That's how we felt about it and we see no point in concealing it. I have to be true to myself. I want to be *me*." They make it clear that morality is determined by an internal integrity—is in fact a living out of "the way I really am."

These words bring me to the second reason The New Adulterers upset me. They confuse me by their Newspeak. The words used are not always new, but they make them, like Humpty Dumpty, mean something new.

"Honesty," for instance, commonly means paying your way, not stealing and not lying. Its new use goes deeper. It now means in addition, "to strip away false fronts, to let people see how we really are."

If this were all that the new honesty meant, I would be overjoyed. Many of us have failed to be honest in this deeper sense. But the danger is that this same honesty is often only a cover for selfishness, rudeness or cruelty. If I think your face is ugly and I dislike you, does this mean that to be true to myself I must say: "I dislike you. Your face is a disaster!"?

Love may recognize that your face is a catastrophe. But love also will sense your discomfort. Love never wounds unless the wound is for the greater good of the person wounded. And love takes priority over honesty.

Honesty is only one cliché among many of the sexual Newspeak. *Meaningful* becomes meaningless. If you have a meaningful sexual relationship with your neighbor's spouse, you may hold up your head with an air of moral superiority. What you have done is "healthy." It may have contributed to "personal growth" and increased "personhood" or have been a "means of personal development" for both of you. Or so the books say. A little added sharing of one's sexuality can thus be a "maturing experience." Those who use such arguments remind me of Paul's scathing words: "They glory in their shame" (Phil. 3:19).

Beware of being fooled by words. I was living in Lima in 1964 when the late President General De Gaulle of France visited Peru. Behind the beautiful city, climbing the sides of the mountains below which the city nestles, rose an ugly cancerous excrescence. From all over the city you could see the flimsy shacks of the barrios where unspeakable poverty reigned and where thugs and lesser political refugees hid from the police.

Just before De Gaulle arrived a new whiteness glittered in the afternoon sun. Shacks and shanties were transformed overnight to gleam cleanly like quaint Disney World buildings above the city. An army of painters had worked wonders. Only when you got close did you see that only those walls facing the city had been painted white. The barrios remained barrios.

We may whiten adultery with new Sexspeak, but we shall not have changed anything that matters. Nor if we wish to blacken monogomy by calling it "unhealthily rigid" and "unrealistically restrictive" have we done anything more than indulged in academic mudslinging. And neither mudslinging nor whitewashing helps us to see things as they are.

Our goal in sex, as in anything else, is to be free. But before we look at the Scripture on adultery, let us look where the new sexual freedom actually points. Let us not even bother to inspect the Newspeak itself which I have rightly labeled academic whitewashing. Melvin Maddocks puts his finger on the heart of the matter.[2] Freedom is determined by something inside us rather than by external rules.

Joe may feel free to share sexuality with Mary, his friend's bride next door. And Mary may find it "enriching" and "maturing." But for the system to work, a new set of laws even tougher than the Mosaic laws has to be created for Joe's wife, Jane, and Mary's new husband, Jim.

In attempting to ignore morality Joe and Mary have consciously created new moral absolutes which are more difficult to attain than the old biblical ones. If we decide, for instance, that marital partners in open marriages should share their sexuality with other friends, we make new kinds of demands on them. We liberate their behavior in some ways only to restrict it in others.

If it is "right" (that is, "healthy," "maturing," "deeply fulfilling" or whatever supposedly nonmoral adjectives you want to use) for Mary to share her sexuality with the man next door, then it goes without saying that it will be essential for her new husband, Jim, to "be adult" about the matter. He must not give way to primitive feelings of anger or possessiveness.

We have thus added new commandments in the teeth of terrible ancient temptations: Thou shalt not be jealous. Thou shalt not be possessive of thy wife or husband. Thou shalt always be understanding of the wonderful maturing process that thy husband is undergoing in his fascination with thy neighbor Mary.

For we are caught, whether we choose to ignore it or not, in a moral universe. We love, we feel, we hate. God's laws, rightly understood, offer us freedom in that universe, not bondage. Any attempt to change his laws will restrict rather than increase our freedom as we grapple with the conflict between reality around and the raging of our passions within.

That freedom is the truest which most closely conforms with our true nature: and our true nature is that which God made, designed as it is to harmonize with the universe he set it in.

Three Kinds of Betrayal

The new style adulterers are not the only ones who justify what they do. Just as common is the man who says to me, "Doctor, I don't feel any sense of wrong when we're together. I love her." He looks me squarely in the eye. Honesty in his face represents sincerity in his heart. He loves her. And he really does feel no wrong when they are together—in bed or out. "The only thing I feel bad about is my wife."

You love her? What do you mean? What is love? Sexual attraction? "No doc, not that. Much more than that. She understands me, doc. She makes me feel like a human being. She listens when I talk. She doesn't laugh at me. Sure, she's attractive, but it's not that. I never felt this way about my wife or about any other woman."

Among the Greek words for love, three are outstanding: *eros* (sexual attraction or being "in love"), *philadelphia* (brotherly love) and *agape* (the word which alone describes the unique quality of divine love).

Eros and philadelphia are based on attraction. Agape alone arises from the nature of the lover—that special nature that causes the lover to love equally the unattractive and the attractive. Please notice the huge difference. Jesus loved the leper *because he could not help doing so.* He was and is love. His love was not a response to something in the leper. Such response would be pity, not love.

You experience eros for a man or woman who attracts you sexually and with whom you fall "in love" and philadelphia for the man or woman whose personality draws you into deep bonds of respect and friendship. Both "loves" represent your responses to some stimulus in the person who attracts.

Eros and philadelphia together make a good marriage a possibility. But when to eros and philadelphia agape is added, you have the marriage that no power can break.

Eros and philadelphia can both betray sworn oaths of commitment. The eros that attracted me to my husband may later attract me to another man for whom I may in addition begin to experience philadelphia. Or the philadelphia that attracts me to that warm-hearted woman at the office may later be mixed with eros. And as my philadelphia and eros for her grow, so my "love" for my wife will wane.

But all the eros and philadelphia in the world do not justify the betrayal of an oath. For the betrayal of an oath is the betrayal of a person. It is not copulation that is the "wicked" thing in betrayal. Copulation is good (just as apples are good). It is stealing and cheating that make adultery bad, not copulation. A stolen apple can be sweet and eating it a profoundly healthful experience. Never in my life have I tasted anything so *good* as trout we caught by poaching on the Isle of Skye once. We cooked them on the shore on a fire of driftwood as the sun went down and the blue-green waves pounded the rocky beach. My heart was light and full of joy. I did not really feel bad about the poaching. But our enjoyment of the poached trout did not make poaching right. How much less do eros and philadelphia (the combination we call "love") justify the treachery of adultery.

"But doctor, it must be right because it feels so beautiful. Something so lovely just could not be wrong." An attractive woman, she sat tensely on the edge of her chair, twisting a handkerchief tightly around her fingers.

Is that which feels beautiful right? How much are feelings about beauty to be trusted when it comes to gambling with our own and other people's lives? Is not that how the whole trouble started? "So when the woman saw that the tree was good for food, and that it was a delight to the eyes, and that the tree was to be desired to make one wise, . . ." she was fooled by her feelings ("Adam, dear, it must be all right. It tastes so good.") into choosing death (Gen. 3:6).

"There is a way which *seems* right to a man, but its end is the way to death" (Prov. 14:12, my emphasis). No, dear lady, I know exactly how you feel but you are wrong. Your feelings have betrayed you.

You see, what is right (really right, deep in the very core of righteousness) does feel good. Even in pain it fills a man with a joy that makes all other joys cheap imitations. But though what is right feels good, it does not follow that all that feels good and beautiful is right.

"But doctor, my marriage has failed. There is absolutely nothing left in it. Surely I am not to be blamed for what I am doing."

Forty-year-old Joan, mother of three teen-age children, was grateful for her job as a nursing instructor. She badly needed the steady income and the absence of shift work. John, her husband, an occasional social drinker, had slowly turned their life of eighteen years together into a nightmare (or so it seemed to Joan). Joan could not say at what point she had realized he was an alcoholic.

Was it after their first major car accident? Or was it the second time he had disappeared for several days? Most of the memories, like the loud embarrassing exits from cocktail parties or the time when John had to be carried to the car, were forgettable. But there were others that were not—like the vicious telephone calls from an unknown woman; the endlessly unpayable bills; the lost jobs; the badgering from credit stores; the time the light, heat and telephone were cut off in the same month; the time the children stood in a huddle and cried, not because they were hungry, but because daddy was kicking mommy's bedroom door down; and finally the first time she told them at work that her black eye came from tripping over one of the children's toys on the basement stairway.

When Joan had decided to stick it out, she had been helped by her local minister, a man trained in counseling and in the ways of alcoholics. His car was often available when she needed it. But it was Pastor Bill's counsel that sustained her. Through him she found Christ—a real person who became her Savior and Lord.

Pastor Bill would listen patiently as the embittered and bewildered thoughts spilled from her. He said little, but what he did say had taught her to face her failures squarely and had given her strength and purpose outside herself.

It came as a shock to realize one day that Pastor Bill, the man who had led her to Christ, strong, reliable, wise Pastor Bill, was not without his own troubles. His bedridden, paralyzed and rather petulant wife, and his need to care for home, meals and the many responsibilities of the church all contributed to his vulnerability. Not that he asked for pity as one by one the details of his own burdens came to light. He wanted her to know that in some obscure way Joan's presence at their weekly sessions had helped him as much as they seemed to have helped her. She was glad to know that it could be so. She promised to pray. It made her debt to him that much less. She was also surprised to realize how happy it made her just to enjoy talking with him and to know that she could give back to him a measure of the strength he had given to her.

What began as a plea for help and an outpouring of pain became a sharing of mutual difficulties and a source of prayerful encouragement. A man and a woman found increasing strength in each other, strength to face difficult days in their respective homes. Gratitude and respect grew to friendship and friendship to affection.

The steps by which that same affection deepened and was expressed physically are of little consequence. What is important is that both, after heart searching, decided they were doing no wrong. There was a dimension in their relationship entirely lacking from both their marriages, a union that had a "meant to be" quality about it. No one who had not shared their circumstances had the insight, let alone the right, to judge.

John refused to divorce Joan and somehow she was able to cope with the house and her children's needs. Bill stuck by his invalid wife. No one, so far as they could determine, knew anything about their affair.

The details of no two stories are the same, but their essences are. In many case histories nagging wives, cruel husbands and unfaithful marital partners (who have "never understood me") figure prominently. Yet when all due allowance is made for the immaturity and selfishness on the part of those who seek sexual companionship outside their marriages, it remains true that many people's extramarital affairs might be justifiable if marriage were no more than a valuable social convention or a practical family partnership.

The people involved wish things had worked out differently in their cases. But their special circumstances lie beyond the scope of rigid laws. Their marriages are hollow, to be preserved "for the sake of the children" or because divorce for one reason or another is out of the question. And since the loving support of the adulterous relationship somehow holds things together and preserves the sanity of some of the involved parties, it seems justified. What would be wrong for people in general becomes right for those in marital trouble.

There are several moral problems in such arguments. Just how much marital difficulty justifies adultery? Where on the spectrum ranging from a warm, wholesome marriage to a cold, hostile one does the point come that justifies an affair? If Joan, beaten (she had tried to leave John twice but had taken him back on his tearful promises to reform), embattled with creditors, and badgered with lies, abuse and disgusting behavior from her husband, is justified, who else is? And how does one go about deciding?

If you have any feelings at all, you should at this point either be angry (with me perhaps) or sickened with heartache. I do not know what your own involvement with adultery or with people caught in adultery might be. But if it has been like mine, you will have groaned and wept at the years of hopelessness, fear, suspicion, bitterness and pain inextricably tangled in extramarital affairs.

But I am a doctor. I must be compassionate, but I must not lie. I cannot pretend that cancer is not cancer. To do so is not being compassionate—it is a betrayal. It is a betrayal of my profession and of the patient who came to me with his trust. And in the same way I cannot pretend that adultery is sometimes okay because the circumstances that led to it were unspeakably tragic. My business is not to judge at all. My business is to tell it like it is and (where I am asked to do so) to try to help.

Do I need to do more than quote the seventh commandment: Thou shalt not commit adultery? I have no intention of defending the seventh commandment. It needs no defense. But the Bible itself makes clear in many places how and why adultery is wrong. I have already dealt with one of the reasons (the betrayal of trust, the breaking of a lifelong covenant). This holds for Christians and non-Christians alike. A society where covenants can have new clauses added at the whim of either party to the covenant is a society doomed to disintegrate.

But for the Christian the matter becomes crystal clear. Marriage reflects the relation between Christ and his church (Eph. 5:25-33). Is it conceivable that Christ would "commit adultery" because his bride the church were to prove (as she so often has) unfaithful? For the Christian need anything more be said?

Why Does the Water Boil?

What behavioral scientists prefer to describe as "extramarital relationships" are "explained" in a number of ways. I put explained in quotes to remind myself that though we think we explain human behavior, we really only succeed in describing one aspect of it.

To ask why someone commits adultery is like asking why water boils. I cannot give you a simple answer to the question, Why is the water in the kettle boiling? I can only supply you with several answers, answers of different orders. I can say, for instance, "It boils because when water reaches a temperature of 100 degrees centigrade at normal atmospheric pressure, it begins to turn into vapor." But I have not told you *why* the water boils. I have only described what happens when water reaches a temperature of 100 degrees centigrade. I could give you a more complicated discription involving energy transfer and the relations between molecules in liquids and vapors, but I would still be describing rather than explaining.

On the other hand I could say, "The water is boiling because I switched on the stove." This would be a different order of explanation than the scientific one. Everything depends on what I am asking when I ask, Why?

I mention the point because in explaining sexual behavior in scientific or psychological terms, what is known as *determinism* creeps in. Science is built on cause and effect relationships, the idea that cause A automatically brings about result B. If I drop china on cement, the cement causes the china to break. But in explaining human behavior we must beware of assuming that adultery is as inevitable as the breaking of china on cement given certain conditions. A point, it is true, may be reached when we lose control of our behavior, but that point is not reached before we have placed ourselves there. We are all responsible for what we do. We are not machines.

Why then look at the psychology of adultery? I do so because it may help us to understand why it is more of a temptation to some people than to others. And understanding opens the door to compassion.

At the beginning of the book we began to see that sex was intended to end aloneness. It is a bridgeway to communion and fellowship. We also saw that the communion (the closeness, the intimacy, the knowing-and-being-known, the loving-and-being-loved) was a complex living structure that takes years to grow. It begins as a delicate and beautiful plant, vibrant with life. It grows into a sturdy tree with deep roots to sustain it through drought and storm.

Yet you know as well as I do that many marriages do not have communion that has grown like a sturdy tree. The plants never grew. Deep needs in both partners are not being met. And in each partner's heart exists a need to find what he or she truly needs.

What could be more natural, then, than to look outside the marriage for what is not being found within it? And though physical sex figures so prominently in our minds when we think of adultery, it often plays a less important role than the feelings of people engaged in it. "It's not the physical sex," as one woman put it. "It's a feeling I get that he really cares about me. He makes me feel appreciated. I'm never lonely when we're together." Thus in the place of the tree that did not grow, a new plant has come to life in response to a deep urge to know and be known.

A person's need for closeness may make itself felt under many circumstances. Long separation, the death of a husband or wife and a divorce all may cause it to do so. All are therefore circumstances which make extramarital relationships easier to form.

But other questions arise. Every married person at some time faces long periods of loneliness, and many go through bereavement and divorce without committing adultery. Many people go through lonely rituals of marriage without ever looking outside their empty marriages for fulfillment. Why do some people commit adultery and not others?

Beliefs about the rightness and wrongness of adultery seem to be of less importance than we often think. Beliefs themselves can change remarkably under the pressure of need. And even where they remain unchanged, a person may still become an unhappy, conscience-smitten victim of a relationship he cannot give up.

Sex and Self-Respect

Some people seem trapped and seem to trap others by the personalities they are saddled with. Jenny, a dramatic, histrionic woman in her middle forties, leans forward as she talks to me, her wide eyes looking beseechingly into mine. She pours out a remarkable story. She exaggerates. At times I am not sure if she is lying or if she really believes what she says. Her body movements give subtle hints that she and I could have a relationship other than the purely professional one we are now engaged in. But I know that if I were to touch her hand she would slap me indignantly or run crying from the office.

She "can't stand" sex. "I can't bear to have my husband touch me," she says, as she moves close enough for me to smell the perfume that arises from her visible cleavage. "I wish I could. I try but I can't stand it."

She has had many affairs (involving physical sex), but all of them turned sour. Each story sounds the same. Only the names of the men change. In each case the physical sex seemed more important to the man than to Jenny. She would begin by enjoying it, but later, as with her husband, she had become increasingly frigid.

How do we explain this strangely contradictory woman? With her eyes, her eyelids, her dress, her movements she seems to give all men the come on. Yet those who accept her body's invitations are either repulsed or accepted for a time and then rejected. "All men are the same," she complains. "They only want one thing."

But Jenny, it is you who offer it to them. Me doctor? Me? I *hate* sex I tell you! Then why Jenny, do you wiggle your hips when you walk? Why the miniskirt? Why do you flutter your eyelids, then open your eyes wide and stare right into mine? Why the contradiction between your body language and your words?

Why indeed?

The tragic fact is that Jenny never understood her father. She wanted, as a tiny girl, to know and be loved by this enigmatic and sometimes frightening man. She has no clear memories of it now, though at the time she succeeded in discovering how to charm him. She learned at three or four to flutter her eyelashes, to walk with a precocious wiggle of her rear end, to look round coyly at daddy, to tease and to flirt. She discovered that these little actions, meaningless to her, changed his mood. He would laugh, wrap his big arms around her and place her in the warm safety of his lap. There was no place like daddy's lap. She felt secure and protected when she was close to him.

But those times were promises of a friendship that never ripened, a solid relationship between father and daughter that never came into being. His moods changed with the suddenness of tropical storms. She could never be sure of him, never understand him.

She has never been sure of any man since. She is telling the truth when she says she does not enjoy sex. You can enjoy sex if you are sure of yourself or if you trust and understand the other person. Jenny is sure of nothing and no one. Her life is a bitter search for love, not sex. And since a loving relationship with someone of the opposite sex has to be learned first with a parent (and Jenny never learned it), she has no idea how to find it now. All she has is the wrong key, the key that earned her the only love and security she ever knew—on daddy's lap.

Throughout her life she has been using that key to open doors to disappointment. Women either envy or despise her. Men find her fascinating but frustrating. Jenny, alone and bewildered among them all, continues her endless search with the only thing she has, her useless key of a sexual provocation she does not even understand.

But Jenny's story illustrates one of many ways in which early experiences may, like present loneliness, pave the pathway to adultery. Consider another.

Last night I talked with a twelve-year-old girl who was waiting outside a bar for her father. Brothers and sisters—yes, she had seven. The youngest, aged one, lived in a city many miles away. Was he staying with her grandparents? "Oh, no. He's with daddy's girl friend." The phrase slipped out with a total absence of self-consciousness or embarrassment.

Millions of children are growing up accepting the marital unfaithfulness of adults as a simple fact of life. This can work two ways. The pain it causes can give a child a determination to build a different kind of life (though not necessarily the equipment to build it with), or it can again make it all the easier, when the time comes, for them to follow the example that has throughout their lives been so familiar.

Jenny would be labeled "a hysterical personality" by some social workers. But her main problem is in essence not too different from that of many men and women who in later life are in no way hysterical personalities. Some have never been certain of their masculinity or femininity. As their powers of attractiveness wane in middle age, they look for some kind of reassurance that they are still desirable, attractive. So middle-aged men have affairs with their secretaries. And middle-aged women seduce young unmarried men.

There is a mistaken belief, you see, that *increased* virility is the cause of adultery. All the evidence points in the opposite direction. So often it is doubts about one's attractiveness or virility that lead to affairs, particularly flirtatious, short-term ones. The man who is forever trying to lay women is usually a man trying to reassure himself about his unconscious doubts. Naturally he will deny this. So far as he is concerned he is in pursuit of pleasure. But his very boasting and the relish with which he regales his friends with his conquests tells us, without having any profound understanding of psychology, that he is *anxious to be known as* a red-blooded man. He protests too much. His very boasting is the index of his inner doubt, and the pleasure he gets from his sport is enhanced by a needed reassurance about his prowess.

Psychologists, sociologists and psychiatrists on the other hand show increasing interest in what has been called "the identity crisis of middle life." Drs. Prosen and Martin describe in a recent series of articles in *Archives of General Psychiatry* the struggle of the man to whom success has come.[3] His increased wealth and prestige have created the illusion in his mind that he has not lost the physical potential and attractiveness of his youth. New vistas of power excite him. He is bigger and better than he ever dreamed. Why should it surprise him that younger women should be attracted to him? Power excites. If I can leap across some of life's impregnable walls, why not others? Who am I? My life holds more possibilities than I ever dreamed.

But more commonly it is loneliness and the lack of a sense of worth that are the key. Many single professional women live in studio apartments haunted by their dates—married and bachelor. Liberated? Free?

One can only know by talking to them. But those I have talked to discover, as we explore their behavior together (behavior which puzzles and dissatisfies them) that many are the victims of their own sense of worthlessness plus the exploitation of weak, self-pitying men. Aware, in her own words, that she is "being used," she has the painful sense that any worthwhile man would dislike her were he ever to discover what she is really like inside. He would never want her as a wife.

So she pays for the pleasures of the companionship that mitigate her loneliness by giving the one thing her companions will be certain to appreciate about her. She is grateful for the exchange even though she may be aware that the protestations of love and appreciation she gets are hollow.

And where did her sense of worthlessness come from? Again as we look back into her childhood we may discover at least part of the explanation. Her parents provided well for her body but not for her need of approval. She could never meet their expectations. Her father in particular was impossible to satisfy. When her report card bore an A, his only comment would be that if she had tried harder she would have gotten an A plus. Slowly she came to live with the feeling that she was substandard, especially when her father (and later other men) were around.

But the big question that remains is, How do we help an adulterer who cries to us for help as well as the "wronged" partner who has been betrayed?

As Fantasy Relates to Divorce

If there be by any chance someone reading these lines who prays, "I thank thee Lord that I am not as other men are, adulterers, unclean, . . ." know that this chapter is for all of us. Let me show you how.

In the Sermon on the Mount Jesus links in the most curious way two sexual topics which seem poles apart. In Matthew 5: 27-32 his theme is one. Yet as we read the paragraph we instinctively try to divide it into watertight compartments. For he begins by talking about sexual fantasies (lusting after someone sexually in one's imagination) and immediately follows up the thought by denouncing divorce and remarriage. He connects the two by saying in effect that both (sexual fantasies and remarriage after divorce) constitute adultery.

We squirm as we read the passage, adding mental footnotes to explain "what it really means." Skewered on the piercing sword of what it might be saying, we do all we can to get rid of the sharp edge of his words.

The paragraph must be understood in the light of the whole Sermon. One of the things Jesus is doing is claiming to give an authoritative interpretation of the law. Whenever we truly encounter the Word of God, we are shocked. That which reveals God is too frightening. The blinding light shows the messy, dirty clutter of our lives, so that like housewives caught with an untidy house when an unexpected visitor calls, we hasten to explain our innocence.

The scribes and Pharisees had, in spite of their fanatical zeal for law, invented a system by which they could live comfortably with it. They "interpreted" it. The law was aimed at one's actions in order to reveal *what was in the heart.* Its purpose was to awaken the conscience; and the Pharisees had protected their consciences from the law by a thousand subtle interpretations of specific laws which evaded the spirit of those laws while creating for the Pharisees the delusion that they were pleasing God by keeping it to the letter.

Jesus in his Manifesto of the Kingdom cuts through the

mass of erudite nonsense by which the theologians of generations had evaded the thrust of the law and gets at the spirit behind it. In effect he is saying, "Far from destroying the law, I want to show you what its commands really mean." (He did not only fulfill the law by living a perfect life and by meeting the Father's every demand upon him, he also did it by revealing in his teachings the standard that God demands of all.) If we understand this, we shall better be able to appreciate his comments on sexual fantasies, divorce and remarriage.

Most of us know what it is to be stirred sexually by someone of the opposite sex. If we are normal (I do not even say sinful), it is inevitable that we shall be from time to time. We may not be greatly stirred. It may only be a moment's pleasurable appreciation of the attractiveness of another person. Or again it may hit us powerfully in a breathless uprush of desire.

Whether the pleasurable stirring or the overwhelming uprush becomes what Jesus calls lust, really depends on how we handle it. There is nothing wrong with being tempted. Even Jesus "in every respect has been tempted like as we are" (Heb. 4:15). Temptation becomes sin when we give way to it.

We all know Luther's quip about not being able to stop birds flying around our heads but being well able to stop them building nests in our hair. And what Jesus is teaching us is that there is more than one way of responding to sexual temptation. I can say, "Thank you, Lord, for alerting me of the danger. Thank you for the gift of being capable of sexual desire; but thank you, too, for reminding me that this (man or woman) is not for me. Do your will in my heart now as I yield its control to you." Incidentally, he always speaks loudly and clearly. If you have not noticed this, it is because the voice of God has become one of the background noises of your life, noises which you have trained yourself to screen out.

Another way of responding would be to give way to temptation and attempt to seduce the attractive person. Some men and women do this with the full awareness of what they are doing. Others, as we have seen already, do so but fool themselves with a lot of nonsense about meaningful relationships.

But there are other ways still. Some of us do not seduce because we lack the courage to. We are too cowardly. We fool ourselves into feeling we are better than others because our bodies have never been united with any other bodies than those of our spouses; when in fact the real reason behind our virtue is that we just do not have what it takes to have an affair. So we drool virtuously, casting a lustful eye here and there, enjoying the secret delights in the brothels of our hearts.

I would like to make a distinction here. I do not know how valid it is but I think it bears on what Jesus is saying. In the chapter on masturbation, and in a subsequent chapter mentioning voyeurism, the problem of sexual fantasies raises itself. It seems to me that it is one thing to allow my fantasies to be stirred by the cover of a pornographic magazine and something altogether different to allow myself to play lustfully with the idea of having a relationship with a flesh and blood man or woman whom I know personally. Both activities are fantasy activities. Yet it seems to me that in Matthew 5 it is the second of these that Jesus is talking about.

I must be careful not to make too much of the distinction for in real life it is less clear-cut than in my example. Halfway between the nude in *Penthouse* or *Playgirl* and the person I know in real life comes the girl in the bikini on the beach. The girl in the magazine is not (to me) a person. But then neither, for that matter is the bikinied body on the beach.

Yet the distinction remains an important one. Sexual fantasies stimulated by pornography are purely erotic fantasies. They have to do with physical, animal arousal only. The masturbating adolescent, obsessed with the breasts of a pinup and torn with an urge in his groins is thinking primarily of his own physical feelings and the desire to relieve them. But the sexually experienced man or woman (whether young or old), those who know what is involved in a sexual relationship and especially those who may be involved in an unsatisfactory marriage relationship, are in a different position. Their prime preoccupation is with the grass in another meadow which seems greener than the grass in their own. Or else it may be the man or woman who has no pasture but covets what belongs to another. John speaks of the "lust of the eyes," the desire to possess beautiful things. Lust exists where our desires are our masters rather than our servants. So that to lust after a woman has a broader meaning than merely to experience erotic arousal.

I am not seeking to justify playing around with sexually stimulating fantasies. To play around with sexual fantasies is a miserable, guilt-evoking, lonely travesty of sex. I do not believe, however, that sexual fantasies in general are what Jesus is talking about (for reasons which will become still clearer later). He is talking rather about coveting another person's spouse, or else someone known to me whom I may not possess.

And if Jesus is speaking about coveting someone else's spouse, it becomes a little clearer why he immediately goes on to talk about divorce and remarriage. The sin of adultery lies in a broken covenant. (And remember, the fact that someone broke a promise to me does not justify my breaking a promise to him.) As a sin it falls into the same category as treachery and theft.

What Jesus is saying is that since faithfulness is a matter of the heart, there are different ways in which you can commit adultery. You can do so in the conventional sense; or, lacking the courage, you can tease yourself with lust for a person you cannot have; or you can make use of those Mosaic laws designed to protect the rights of a wronged woman, that is, you can get rid of your spouse "legally" and marry someone else. Thus adulterers, lusters and at least some remarried divorcees are all in the same boat. It is a very large boat. Let us beware of pointing fingers at one another when we may be sailing together in it.

I recognize that in treating the passages I do, I am evading many ethical and moral aspects of divorce and remarriage. I do so deliberately since these aspects lie beyond the scope of this book. You will notice that in the paragraph above I said "at least some" remarried divorcees. Frankly, I do not know about all of them. But if the cap fits, why not wear it? You who are divorced and remarried (yes, happily remarried—but what of that? God makes the sun to shine on the just as well as the unjust), are you really as righteous as you make yourself out to be? Are you that much better than the rest of us? Or are you playing the Pharisees' game of twisting the Scriptures to justify your past selfishness?

I write as I do not to get at you and certainly not to suggest that your present marriage should be dissolved. What is done is done. It cannot and should not be changed. If you have acted righteously, well and good. But if (and this is true of many of you) your remarriage was the end product of a wrong and sinful pathway, then face it. Until forgiveness and cleansing can reach this area of your life, your fellowship with God will be incomplete.

Can Things Be Put Right?

This chapter is not on marriage counseling. It is to help people involved in sexual sin and in particular with those men and women having extramarital affairs.

Let me begin, you who want help, with the problem that has so often been put to me. You realize you must give her (him) up. But you cannot stop feeling. You say (and you mean it) that the affair has got to finish. It has cost you a lot to come to the decision, but now you know you must quit.

You also tell me, sadly, that things can never be the same again. Having tasted the warmth and joy of your extramarital relationship, your marriage is going to seem flat. You are willing to be faithful, but how can you tell your spouse "I love you." when you feel no love? You do not hate her (him). You may not even dislike her (him). But you do not feel for your spouse what you felt for your lover. And you have no heart to put on an act.

96

You say something else. "I will never see my lover again. But I can't forget her either. I'll always feel the same way."

Some people would be shocked if you were to tell them this. They do not understand that eros and philadelphia, even if sinful, are real. Their roots penetrate the hearts of men and women. The fact that neither of you had any right to let them grow makes no difference. They cling deeply in the soil of your being. Confessing your sin and abandoning your lover have not altered this.

How real is your renunciation? Very real?

I believe you. What is about to happen to you is what happens to people who lose a loved one in death. It could crush the survivor if God had not placed within us all the mechanisms needed to deal with the inflicted wounds of death. Such a person goes through a process called by some psychiatrists "the work of grieving." Grief work is a God-given mechanism to heal the deep wounds of the attachments uprooted from our lives. It has recognizable stages involving, in different people, feelings of numbness, bouts of sighing, a tendency to weep, poor sleep, feelings of depression and sometimes of resentment, the slow changing of the quality of the memories of the departed one, then gradually, the capacity to form new attachments to replace the old. But the process cannot be hurried. It takes time.

Max, a thirty-five-year-old dentist, came into my office six months after quitting an affair with his receptionist. His wife knew all about it. His pastor and the deacons in the church knew. He had resigned his own position as a deacon. Like so many he had originally told me, "I just am not going to be able to pretend, doctor. I'll never see Lydia again, but I'll never be able to forget her either. I don't feel any love for my wife at this point." We worked through his immediate feelings for several sessions and then for some weeks I did not see him.

Not so long afterward his face seemed five years younger. There was a quizzical, half-puzzled smile on his face. "I have a feeling you know what I am going to say," he began. "It's happened. The Lydia thing seems like a dream. And I actually do love my wife. I can't explain what's happened. . . ." He paused. "It's as though I've woken up from a sort of nightmare. Our marriage has never been so good. Sure, we argue sometimes. But we are talking now. We have learned to work things out. The kids are happier—and I'm enjoying them."

"We are talking now. . . ." They had not been—not just since the affair started but for years before. They had exchanged courteous words about the house, the children, money, the church, their future. They even prayed together. Both were graduates of a well-known Bible college. Sometimes Max had shouted when he was angry. But more important than what was said were the many things left unsaid. The things Max shouted about were really the things that he resented most deeply about his wife. In his own words, "I didn't want to hurt her." And in the slow accumulation of unspoken resentments, their verbal exchanges served as a curtain between them. The two became actors going through the motions of marriage. The stage was set for Max's affair with Lydia years before it began.

So in addition to the healing process God is going to do in your heart, something else must happen. You are going to have to learn to talk—about your real feelings and resentments. This will be risky. But you can never really have a relationship unless you are willing to risk losing it. A marriage that consists of walking on eggshells is no marriage. If the risk of opening up seems too great, then seek professional help from a good marriage counselor. From the outset of this book I have striven to show that sexuality in its broadest sense has to do with the ending of aloneness. God created sex for that purpose. And the healing of a broken marriage must also begin with the deliberate opening up of new channels of communication.

The Secret Affair

"But doctor, my wife knows nothing about my affair. It's over now. I want to tell her about it. Should I?" Here, indeed, is a problem of communication. Should everything be shared? In particular should this man share his problem and sin? "If my husband had an affair, I never want to know about it!" Many women have told me this emphatically. But they do not speak for all women.

Is there any question as to what a Christian ought to do? Can a Christian marriage continue with a buried secret?

Yet what makes us *want* to confess an episode of unfaithfulness? Some (usually those who have been involved in a brief, casual affair) want to "confess" because of an unconscious urge to hurt their wives or husbands. Sometimes this urge has driven them into the affair in the first place. In such cases "confession" can be an attempt to add insult to injury under the guise of piety and honesty. And no better way can be chosen to inflict deep wounds upon the husband or wife than to confess, from such motives, an affair the spouse knew nothing about.

There is no "right" solution in this case. The man or woman facing such a prospect must inevitably choose between two evils: one of wounding viciously from pious malice and the other of bearing within them the weight of a sin that they cannot share with the person who should be closest to them. Therefore be sure before God of your motives before you speak.

Share the problem first with some godly counselor whose spiritual integrity you can trust. He might advise that you remain silent at least for the moment. Silence in such a case does not imply that you must lie if your spouse questions you. One day you may have to own up. And though the shock of the discovery in answer to his question will be great, and the doubts it will raise in his mind be many, you can at least in that case take him by the hand to the counselor to whom you opened your heart, and say to him: "Now I want you to tell my husband all I told you."

The "Injured Party"

"It's been going on for at least three years. I knew something was wrong but she kept denying it. We'd been fairly close friends with the other couple—gone on picnics with them, visited—you know. Sometimes I didn't like the way they looked at each other. Has it all been my fault, doctor? What do I do now?" He was a thirty-nine-year-old professor of anthropology. His pathetic bewilderment was that of a little boy. But the bent shoulders and lines in his face belonged to a man much older than thirty-nine.

"We've had it all out. All four of us. I blame his wife more than anyone else. She is a masochistic, sanctimonious martyr. I can't blame him for hating her. Just now I feel depressed. But sometimes I'm enraged. And the worst of it all is that I can't be sure it's not still going on. Jill denies anything. But then she always did deny it until the final showdown.

"It came out then. But some of the details don't check. I keep wanting to ask more questions. Have they really told us how many times they were together? How often did they have sex? Where did they do it? What did they do? I am obsessed with details—dates, times. . . .

"And when I ask her, she says she can't remember. She says the events just run together and one time was just like another, that it was being loved that mattered. She gets mad when I question and tells me to quit and just leave her alone. The other day flowers arrived for her and when I asked her about them she screamed at me. Somehow there's no end to it.

"We've started having sexual relations again. But," he hesitated and hung his head, "she wants me to do it differently now." He described some of the love play she had persuaded him to engage in.

"Suddenly I had no heart for it. Where did she learn all that? I could see them in my mind's eye doing *that* sort of thing together."

Mistrust, fear, anger, insecurity, bitterness.

I know you are going through pain. Few people know what

you are facing. But do you *want* to build your marriage again? Do you want to learn to trust? If she gets mad because you ask about the flowers, then point out that if she has nothing to feel guilty about, there is no reason for either of you to be upset. Tell her that you know that mistrust is your problem but that you are going to need her help if you are to get over it.

Your obsession with details, however—watch that! Jill probably does not remember every detail about every sex act. Why should she even want to? What are you trying to do to her, extract every last juicy morsel of sin on the rack of your inquisition? Are you playing Christ at the judgment seat with your wife as the sinner? Tell me, Is your questioning drawing you closer to her or driving you further apart? What will you gain by putting together each piece in the ugly mess of the jigsaw? For you are right, you never *will* know every detail. There *will* be no end to it if you never stop questioning. If you must share things together (and you must), share those things that will draw you closer, your inmost joys and sorrows, the children's activities.

But about forgiveness? Yes I know you say you have forgiven her, but what have you forgiven? Only what you know about? That is not enough. You must make it clear to her that you forgive everything, even the things she cannot remember.

And is it not possible that she feels (in spite of her outer defensiveness) that what she has done will mean that she can never expect to be totally and freely accepted by you again? In a way there is a limit to what you can do about that. Until she can know God's forgiveness, in the depths of her being (a work that only the Holy Spirit can do in her), until she can look on herself with the same kindness and acceptance as God looks on her, she will never be really sure how *you* feel about her.

But you can help. You can help by letting her see that so far as you are concerned the past is the past. You can help by admitting that you failed to make her feel like a woman, and by asking her to teach you how to. You can help by not pushing her. You can help by showing that you understand her grief over what she has lost. Yes, I know that sounds impossible. But it is not. And if you are to win her affection you must pay the price of understanding how she feels. Take your rage to God, and let him show you the wounds of his Son. Then let him teach you compassion for your wife's loneliness.

Have you read the book of Hosea recently? Take a few tips from chapters two and three.

Do not put her on a pedestal. She will feel uncomfortable if you do. Let her know that you accept what has happened and that her weakness as well as your neglect were a part of it. But let her understand that whatever she is, weak or not, you are in no position to condemn her.

You look depressed as I say this to you. You ask me, "Was it my fault?" I am not in the judging business but, yes, you were at least partly to blame. But so what? Your temptation at this point is to lie down in despair, despair at what seems an impossibly steep climb in not only forgiving your wife (husband) but in meeting the need you feel she has no right to have; despair, still more at your own failures of the past and the bitter self-blame that saps strength from every muscle in your body.

Let us stop right there. Did you not know that God was waiting to flood your spirit, soul and body with forgiveness *now*? I mean forgiveness *for you*. Total forgiveness. Of every failure, every sin, every inadequacy on your part. Forget about your spouse for a moment. You cannot be any help to him/her when you cannot drag one foot after another yourself. You cannot bubble with forgiveness in laughing fountains of love unless you yourself are swept up in the tingling floods of God's forgiveness. All God asks of you at the moment is the will to forgive. If you can say (through however much praying) I will, I do forgive, then God demands no more.

He wants to give, and he wants to give to you. Satan the Accuser would have you lie down in despair, piously saying, "I don't have what it takes."

But do not do it. Christ, you see, is the Original Reconciler. He reconciles you to God in himself. He waits, even as you read these words, to let you experience that reconciliation and acceptance through what he has already done in his own death and resurrection.

If he can reconcile mankind to himself, do you suppose that your marriage presents him with any problem? The only problem is that the reconciliation must begin with you. And it can begin now. Do you honestly see yourself as in need of forgiveness? Do you mean it when you say that you are inadequate? Or are you secretly hoping that you are adequate? Are you sure you are sincere when you say you long to know God's total, laughing, loving acceptance of you—just as you are?

Then do as I have sometimes done. Write down a list of the sins and failures you know you are guilty of. Write down some with a question mark if you are not sure whether they are really sins or failures or not. Then take the list, kneel down and meditate on the following sentences from the Bible.

If we say we have no sin, we deceive ourselves, and the truth is not in us. If we confess our sins, he is faithful and just, and will forgive our sins and cleanse us from all unrighteousness. (1 Jn. 1:8-9)

Therefore, brethren, since we have confidence to enter the sanctuary by the blood of Jesus, by the new and living way which he opened for us through the curtain, that is, through his flesh, and since we have a great priest over the house of God, let us draw near with a true heart in full assurance of faith, with our hearts sprinkled clean from an evil conscience and our bodies washed with pure water. (Heb. 10:19-22)

I cannot for want of time and space, explain every detail of these sentences, but I must mention one or two points. The word *sprinkled* refers to sprinkling with blood. The word *blood* refers to the blood of Jesus Christ. Naturally that blood is no longer available in a physical sense. When the Bible speaks of blood it is speaking of death, violent death, sacrificial death. By his blood (death) Jesus canceled the debt of our sins and failures. His death is the only price God demands for your sins and failures. What is more, to offer God anything in addition to Christ's death is to say that Christ's death is not enough. Nothing could be a more terrible insult than to hold Christ's death in such contempt as to say it is inadequate for your special case.

The only other word I wish to comment on is *confidence*. You are instructed to enter boldly into God's presence because you may expect a warm welcome there. You are accepted not because of your spirituality, your tears, your nobility, your contrition or for any other positive or negative quality you may have. You will be accepted because God is love, and he can accept you with all your sin and failure because he accepts you for Christ's sake. Christ's work, if you will only believe enough to act on my words, cancels out everything sinful and negative about you so far as God is concerned.

So write "Canceled" across your list. Step confidently across the threshold into the welcoming arms of the Father. Tell him, if you have to, that you find it all hard to believe. But step forward boldly for the welcoming arms are there.

Then the miracle can begin. The miracle of a burden that lifts, the wonder of joy that you know that you are loved and forgiven. It is a miracle in many senses, but a miracle that can grow like a living thing in your marriage as you allow God's acceptance of you to become your acceptance of your spouse: his forgiveness of you, your forgiveness of the one closest to you, his welcoming arms—the ones whereby you open, not just your physical body, but your very heart to the person who needs you most.

6
Two Halves
Do Not
Make
One Whole

A homosexual act is one designed to produce sexual orgasm between members of the same sex. A homosexual is a man or woman who engages in homosexual acts.

I have chosen my definitions carefully. They put the emphasis where it belongs—on behavior rather than on people, on acts more than on the man or woman who do them, on lifestyles people adopt not on the people who adopt them.

Experts and nonexperts may disagree with me. To many people a homosexual is *a certain kind of person,* a person innately different from the rest of us. He or she may be described as "a queer," "a gay," "a fairy," "a queen," "a homo," the implication usually being that the homosexual lives a homosexual life "because of the way she is." She makes love to a girl for the reason a fish swims; she is acting according to her true nature and doing the thing she was meant to do (or else the thing she cannot help doing—depending on how you look at it). This is all true. But I feel it is only half of the story, the other half of which is neglected in most literature on the subject.

You will notice I say "she" even though the meaning of my sentence would remain the same had I said "he." This is a concession on my part to women's liberation. "He" is shorter, and from habit I may use it more often where "she" would do equally well. We have no singular pronoun in English which refers equally to a man or a woman. But I am glad to begin by using "she" where "he" would also fit for it reinforces another point in my definitions: Homosexuality is a problem common to both sexes. *Homo* means "alike" or "equal to." It does not refer to maleness. Lesbianism is simply a word used to describe female homosexuality.

But to get back to the distinction between acts and the people who commit them: where should the emphasis lie? The question is a crucial one. Christians say that a person sins because he or she is a sinner. It is not that sinning makes the person a sinner, but that having a sinner's nature makes him sin. The statement, a partial truth, parallels the conventional idea of homosexuality. A male homosexual indulges in homosexual intercourse, according to this view, because he has a homosexual nature that *causes* him to behave as he does.

Practicing homosexuals, behavioral scientists and bigoted haters of homosexuality alike seem strangely united on this point: He does what he does because he is what he is.

But the explanation is too simple. We might also say that Bill, who is an alcoholic, drinks because he cannot help it. He is sick. Drink controls him. Try as he might, he never can and never will quit—at any rate, not until he comes to terms at gut level with his "sickness." And even then many authorities would say he must quit forever. Because he is an alcoholic, Bill will probably not be able to become a moderate drinker. He has an inner problem such that he dare not touch a drop. If he does, he has had it. He does what he does because he is what he is.

But let us look more closely. Was Bill always the way he is now? Was there not a time when he could stop at one drink or go for weeks with the same bottle of Scotch in his liquor cabinet and not even think about it? Thirty years ago no one would have dreamed that Bill would become a lush. It was only twenty years ago that one or two of his friends were a little bothered. But as Bill straightened up after drinking a little too heavily for a weekend or so, even his closest friends were reassured. "Bill doesn't have a problem with liquor," they told themselves. But ten years ago the picture had changed. And today nobody has any doubts.

At what point during the thirty years did Bill become an alcoholic? What would have happened, say, had he joined a teetotaler organization after three years of only occasional social drinking and adopted lifelong abstinence. Could he have stopped then? Almost certainly, yes.

No one is born alcoholic. At what point then do we cease to say that his drinking is turning him into an alcoholic, and start to say his alcoholism is driving him to drink? In this respect, though not to the same extent, alcoholism parallels homosexuality. For instance a pure homosexual (someone who has always indulged in homosexuality and never has had the slightest inclination to anything but homosexual behavior) is only at one end of a broad spectrum. If we assess people by their feelings, their preferences and their behavior, we discover that most people, whether their bodies are male bodies or female bodies, seem to have natures of varying combinations of maleness and femaleness.

Some men are described as "all man" and some women as "extremely feminine" or perhaps "all woman." We imply, when we use such expressions, that other men are in some sense men with a touch of something other than maleness about them (such as preferring music to football or sherry to scotch however masculine they may be in other ways). Simi-

larly some women, in addition to their femaleness, have one
or two male traits about their likes or behavior. And the closer
we look, even at the people we know, the more we begin to see
what many careful studies confirm: that there is not the same
sharp distinction between maleness and femaleness in lifestyle
that there is in our bodies. Most of us would see the biblical
Esau as being more manly *in his temperament* than Jacob his
twin. But their bodies (in spite of Esau's hairiness) were
equally male.

Thus our bodies are (with rare exceptions) completely male
or female. On the other hand our ways of living cover a broad
range, seeming to contain a variety of what have been regarded as male and female tastes and preferences. At what
point then do we call someone homosexual?

Because a woman prefers women for her closest friends
and likes engineering, do we call her a homosexual? Because
a man is not athletic, not a ladies' man, gentle and quiet in his
ways and fond of sculpture, do we see him as on the way to
being a homosexual? Neither the man nor the woman I have
described may ever have experienced a wish for an erotic relationship with a member of the same sex and yet both may be
regarded as objects of mistrust by some of us.

On the other hand a man may be a happily married father
of five children, an elder in the local church, a football en-
thusiast but at the same time be a habitué of sleazy steam baths
and a practicing homosexual. Call him bisexual, if you must,
but to do so may be to play with words. His behavior is homosexual as well as heterosexual.

I do not say that our natures and feelings do not matter.
My point is that we are far too inclined to explain behavior on
the basis of nature rather than nurture and to be obsessed
with what a person is rather than what he does.

When I was in junior high, a young, married Christian
youth worker invited me to stay for a week in his home in the
country. My parents were delighted.

The first night I was there he and I had devotions in our

pajamas on our knees beside the double bed he and his wife normally occupied. My own pajama pants, to my embarrassment, had mysteriously disappeared. My friend's wife, for a reason it never occurred to me to question, was to sleep in a single room. After devotions the Christian youth worker and I got into bed together.

What followed made me feel embarrassed, fearful to offend, helpless, angry and sexually aroused, all at the same time. I was too embarrassed to go on resisting his attempts to seduce. They began so gently as not to seem sexual at all. Then as he proceeded, "Oh come now, you're not scared are you? I always wanted a little brother to love like this. What are you afraid of?"

The shame of it lay in the fact that I found a sexual excitement in me which arose in spite of all my attempts to extinguish it. I knew nothing of what homosexuality was. I only knew that I hated myself for the mixture of anger, guilt, pleasure and shame I experienced, and I hated myself for what was happening. I wished I were miles away. No climax occurred (to me at any rate). After he was asleep I lay awake wondering what God was really like and what he felt about me. Ought I to ask for forgiveness? Forgiveness for what? Was not the youth leader a spiritual man? The more I thought, the more unreal God seemed.

My encounter with the youth leader went on over a couple of years before I was able to break it off. I did all I could to avoid future "holidays," but two more occurred. He seemed to have a deep and genuine affection for me. He would reproach me, at times bitterly, when I failed to answer his weekly letters.

There was something unhealthy about his affection which went deeper than sex. He depended on me for his happiness. His was a need love, not just a giving love. He needed my affection. And so on my young shoulders was placed the burden of keeping a Christian youth leader happy. For me it was a sort of emotional blackmail in which I was hopelessly trapped.

Why, you may ask, did I never tell my parents? Tell them

what? I knew it would be wrong for me to engage in such acts with kids my own age, but this man was a Christian leader. In those days I had no language to describe even the physical thing which he kept trying to do, and I was sickened with shame. As for his emotional clinging to me, I did not even understand it. I bore with silent resentment my parents' gentle rebukes about my unanswered mail and sat down to force myself to write letters I hated.

Before high school (or what in England was called grammar school—the North American equivalent of grades seven to twelve) I noticed that pictures of nude women, and particularly of women's breasts, would excite me. Following my encounter with the youth leader statues and pictures of nude males, especially of male genitals, began to have the same effect. We had no sex education in those days and my only reactions were of mingled delight and guilt. My prayer life grew more confused and unsatisfactory.

It is sometimes said that homosexuality is "caused by" the kind of experience I went through. Perhaps so: But that is not why I described it.

My current sexual life is about as normal as it could be. Gradually over the course of many years the sexual interest in male bodies (which I did not give way to but which for a long time I was bitterly humiliated about) has left me, evaporating like an unhealthy cloud, so that at times were it not for memory I would be puzzled as to how it could ever have been. Over the course of those same years my erotic interest in the female body has grown and sweetened, so that I am moved not only erotically but with a strange feeling of reverence and joy by the sight of a woman's body. (In saying this, I am fully aware that these reactions in no way justify looking with lustful eyes at any woman I get a chance to.)

We must beware of oversimplified notions of what homosexuals are and how and why they behave as they do. Since we shall consider the morality of homosexuality as well as the psychology, sociology and physiology of it, we must see two things from the outset. First, it is unjust to classify people on the basis of their feelings, tastes and impulses as "having homosexual tendencies," "being latent homosexuals," or "having a touch of something homosexual about them."

Homosexual is a morally loaded term. It should be confined to those who engage in homosexual acts. The people we label may have neither the wish nor even the impulse to engage in such acts, and we have no right to besmirch them. On the other hand we must grasp that homosexual behavior is not in any sense inevitable in someone who engages in it. It may be understandable. But no homosexual (certainly no Christian homosexual) has the right to say, "I am not responsible for what I do because my homosexual nature *makes me* do it."

We must also see from a more scientific viewpoint that the relationship between what I do and what I am is a fluctuating, two-way relationship. Once I experience physical pleasure with a member of my own sex, I am more likely to want to experience it again. The more frequently I experience it, the more fixed will the pattern become. What I do determines what I am just as much as what I am determines what I do.

For that very reason the experience of heterosexual pleasure can set a chain reaction going in the opposite direction. Many people plagued by homosexual impulses, and even those who have engaged in homosexual acts, have discovered slowly growing changes in themselves as they experience heterosexual pleasures. But we may need to look at these ideas more carefully later on. It is time, perhaps, to look at the wide variety of homosexual people and at the theories that attempt to "explain" them.

Types of Homosexuality

Few people nowadays are fooled by the old notion that there are "typical" homosexuals (the effeminate man or the aggressive, masculine woman). Even the notion that there are homosexual pairs (the aggressive, masculine woman who pairs up with the clinging, dependent woman; and the supermale homosexual who pairs up with the effeminate man) breaks down when we examine it. The stereotypes exist. Some masculine women are homosexual. But so are a variety of women with widely differing characters.

As for pairing, it varies endlessly. The spectrum ranges from casual one night alliances in which the partners know nothing but each other's first name and preferred techniques to lifelong alliances some of them "sanctified" by a form of marriage. The only generalizations that can be made are that women tend to form longer-lasting alliances than men and that lifelong fidelity seems to be much more rare among homosexuals than among straights.

Lionel Ovesey, the psychoanalyst who invented the term *pseudohomosexual* (one who fears he is a homosexual but isn't), describes differing grades or degrees of homosexuality in men. The range is from men who are exclusively heterosexual through those who have only occasionally had relations with men and whose "preferred mode of behavior is heterosexual" (that is, with women) to those who have never had anything but homosexual relations and are therefore "exclusively homosexual."[1] Somewhere in the middle are men I have already referred to as bisexual. They are often married and with children, leading a gay life on the side. Because secrecy has to cloak their homosexual activities they are known in the gay world as "closet queens."

In prisons, in monasteries, in the armed forces and in scientific expeditions involving only men, "situational homosexuality" occurs. Such men usually revert to heterosexual behavior outside jail or when the expedition ends. In jail the curious situation exists where the domineering, physically tough leader asserts his strength and masculinity by subjecting prisoners to forceful anal intercourse (intercourse using the victim's rectum). Far from being looked down on by other prisoners, he is feared and respected. He proves his masculinity by subjugating not only women but even men.

We have already seen that in homosexual relationships, as

in heterosexual ones some people are passive, attracting sexual seduction. As one man said to me: "I am a passive homosexual—anal type. I like it that way. I always let the other guy do it." But we have also seen that relatively few homosexuals can be so easily classified. Many who are passive in one relationship may be aggressive in another while thousands of homosexuals who frequent gay bars for a one night pickup may be neither passive nor aggressive but simply entering into a mutually satisfactory partnership for an evening's pleasure.

Techniques

Why should I describe what I know about techniques homosexuals use to arouse one another? If you are a homosexual, you will know most of them already. If you are not, the information will do you no good.

My only reason for touching briefly on the matter is to awaken in those of us who have no sympathy with homosexuality, some awareness of the desperation to which their tragedy has brought them.

Most people, for instance, react with revulsion to the thought of a penis being inserted into another man's mouth or worse inside his rectum (one of the techniques used by male homosexuals). The thought of two women each licking her lover's clitoris, or fondling other parts of her body dismays the average married woman. Why then is the homosexual not inhibited by the same revulsion?

Starving people in besieged cities of the past found their mouths watering for such delicacies as boiled rats. In the merciless grip of hunger their feelings changed about what was tempting and inviting and what was not. Though a homosexual's urge in one direction is blocked, his sexual appetite remains. When appropriate circumstances arise, it will affect him powerfully. So we should not be surprised when what might sicken another person may seem exceedingly attractive to the homosexual.

113

Causes of Homosexuality

Already we are in a position to see that no one, simple cause can account for homosexual behavior. But we must at least look at the commoner theories that attempt to explain it.

A domineering mother and a passive, ineffectual father are the villains according to some analytic theories.[2] Certainly many homosexual men describe controlling mothers and passive fathers.[3]

Mother is the one in command. Like a galleon she may sweep through the household in full sail, lesser vessels (husband and children) trailing in her wake. She may be loud of voice, decisive, determined, ambitious that her children do well in life. If there are family arguments, she usually gets her way. She is resented. But she is also needed for she gets things done. The rest of the family wish they had more of a say, but no one is willing to protest enough to challenge her supremacy.

On the other hand her control may be less blatant. She may rule with subtlety but with equal tyranny. Fragile and gentle, she may govern her household by a will of steel, by her moral ascendancy (how skillfully she can put people in their place with a well-chosen phrase!) or even by an appeal to her headaches.

But lest we too quickly assign her the role of villain, we must observe that she is only one of several players. If the supporting cast failed to play their roles in the sick drama, she would be reduced to helpless perplexity.

Her husband supports her by his abdication. He knows only two ways of reacting to her: either by an occasional (but ineffective) explosion of wrath or by retiring to the basement to watch the T.V., to read or to drink. Sometimes he spends more of his free time out of the house than in.

The children may react in different ways as well. But the father-mother model on which they base their reactions is an unhealthy one. They have been denied a day-by-day demonstration of healthy parental behavior. They have also been taught for many years to play the family game in the wrong way and by the wrong rules. How then can they be expected to play it by the right rules when they begin their own families?

Out of the many family interactions one may become specially important. If mother selects one of her sons to be her special confidant, she may lay the groundwork for his future vulnerability to homosexual temptation. He, too, however, must play his part. He must fit into the perplexing pattern she expects of him.

Usually he becomes, not in a physical or sexual but in an emotional sense, the husband she never had. The qualities her husband lacks she subtly teaches her son to acquire. Without realizing what is happening, he learns to dance to her music and to respond to her moods.

For him it is a frustrating process. At times his skill in meeting her emotional needs is rewarding and gratifying. But because he can never give her what she is really (but unconsciously) looking for, he finds himself tied to her in a relationship that frustrates them both. He is her little man, but he can never be a real man with her. He learns passivity where he should be learning aggression.[4] His childhood need to please and keep her happy never leaves him free to be independent. His sexual urges must be driven underground. His masculine assertiveness must be quick to defend her but laid aside when it comes to opposing her. He is tied to his mother's apron string and both of them are the losers for it.

Had he a strong father to support him and to model himself on, things might be different. But, father, remember, is in the basement.

As he grows older, the chosen son sometimes discovers that he is less competent with girls his own age than other boys are. He may feel at home and find companionship with quieter, more introverted boys but be drawn with mingled anxiety and yearning to strong, outgoing, aggressive youths who awaken his admiration. The only women he feels at home with are strong-minded women who are intrigued by the appeal his mother has created in him.

Such a young man is not a homosexual. Nor is he what Freud termed a latent homosexual (vicious and cruel term). If any term fits, it is Lionel Ovesey's term pseudohomosexual (someone who may superficially resemble a homosexual but is not one).

Nevertheless he is more vulnerable to homosexual temptation than other young men might be. He has more learning to do in order to establish a healthy sexual relationship with a woman, and he will find it a tougher job to learn to be a good father.

His deepest problem will be one of loneliness, a loneliness which will drive him in one of several directions. He may stay at home, an aging bachelor, hoping for marriage but finding it strangely elusive, growing increasingly dissatisfied with his relationship with his parents. His sexual solace may be in masturbation or in sexual relations with older women.

But some of you will ask: Is not a homosexual person different physically from other people? Is not it a matter of hormones and genes and chromosomes?[5]

Science has so far searched vainly to find a physical basis for homosexuality. The testes of male homosexuals produce the same range of hormones as those of normal men. The ovaries and other hormone producing glands of homosexual women produce the same proportions of sex hormones as those of normal women. Even more curious, eunuchs (men whose testicles have been destroyed), who in general tend to lose their male characteristics of aggression and sexual interest in women, have been known to retain their potency and to have sexual relations. Scientific evidence seems to suggest that while our sex hormones may account (at least in part) for the fact that we exhibit sexual behavior and that we experience sexual urges, our sex hormones *do not necessarily determine either the kind of sexual behavior we indulge in or the sex of the person we choose as a partner.*

It is true that curious sexual anomalies exist in some

people's bodies. For instance it is possible to have the body cells of a female (with what is known as a female chromosome pattern) yet a body that looks like the body of a man and vice versa. But these are exceedingly rare conditions which have no bearing on our present discussion or on the enormous problems of homosexuality.

The analytic theories that try to account for homosexuality by emphasizing the dominant mother and the passive father are by no means the only ones. In any case they fail to explain why many domineering mothers rear heterosexual children or why apparently normal parents rear children who adopt a homosexual way of life. There is enough truth in the theories to make us weigh them very carefully, but not enough truth for us to see the world only through analytic spectacles.

Already (in the chapter on masturbation) we saw that habit (what behavioral scientists might call reinforced learning) can shape behavior. Let a young person once experience pleasure from sex play with someone of his or her own sex, and the sex play will become that much more appealing the next time. The vulnerability of the mother-dominated young man I described above lies precisely here. Because his sexual urges are (at least temporarily) blocked in one direction, they will more easily find an outlet in the other. And because it is easier for him to form deep intimate relationships with someone of his own sex, his sexual urges may be awakened in that context. The pleasure and relief he experiences from a sexual relationship with another man will "stamp in" this pattern of behavior, making it more natural for him in the future.

And really it matters little how the start is made. His seduction by an older man or by someone his own age, or his forceful confinement to the company of other men in the armed services or in jail may be a factor. But if the pleasure and the relief are such as to outweigh his sense of guilt and shame, he can become as hooked to homosexual pleasure as a smoker to cigarettes, an alcoholic to whiskey or a junkie to heroin.

The important question is not why did it start, but what

should his attitude to it be? And if he wants to quit, how can he go about it?

How Homosexuals Feel about Themselves

There have always been "liberated" segments of society where anything goes. Even in Victorian Britain, aestheticism and art for art's sake created a climate in which it was possible for Oscar Wilde to flout public morals in his open homosexual friendship with a young British aristocrat. But in Wilde's day society reacted. Wilde was publicly vilified and later imprisoned. He died eventually in obscurity and poverty.

During my boyhood homosexuality was a subject about which boys snickered and working-class men grew stern and solemn. But the tide has turned. Since 1954 when the British government set up a departmental committee (the Wolfendon Committee) to examine all aspects of homosexuality in the public interest, there has been a climate of increasing public acceptance of those who choose homosexuality as a way of life.

The sixties and early seventies have witnessed the growth in North America of an organized gay movement, fighting both legal and job discrimination against homosexuals, and aggressively promoting a gay lifestyle. In the small city where I live I know of three gay organizations, two of which are seeking public charters. The largest organization holds monthly banquets, attended by several hundred male and female homosexuals, in the parish hall of a Roman Catholic church whose priest is gay. The banquets do not promote lasciviousness, but they encourage homosexual dancing (that is, dancing with partners of the same sex) and include shows and other social activities.

Homosexual marriages in various forms are commonplace throughout the Western world—their ceremonies, rituals, oaths, banquets, speeches and photograph-taking all weirdly parodying conventional marriage.

Yet homosexuals, by and large, are unhappy people. They

are unhappy because however successful their fight against discrimination may be, they will never gain either understanding or acceptance by the straight world. They are also unhappy because they suffer a more than average share of loneliness and rejection—even at times by their gay friends. If inconstancy and infidelity plague the straight world, they plague the gay world to a far greater degree. For the deepest longing in the heart of a homosexual is the longing all of us experience, the longing to be known, to be loved and to be accepted just as we are and for always.

Eroticism may be important to the homosexual, but it is no more important to him or her than to anyone else. It has precisely the same function as in all of us: that of a pathway to the end of aloneness. And because homosexual alliances, even more than straight alliances, are fragile and subject to change, the disappointments are more frequent and the despair deeper.

In addition, many homosexuals are afraid to come out and join the gay world. Some live double lives, denizens of two worlds, the one straight and the other gay. Their gay friends despise them for their timidity while they live in constant anxiety lest their straight colleagues, friends and families discover what they are doing and shun them.

Drugs and alcohol compound the problem of many, particularly of female homosexuals. Of the homosexual clubs in my city, one has a bar and the other is dry. The first is the one most frequented by women and the other almost entirely used by men.

It has often been said that male alcoholics all have a streak of homosexuality in them. The statement is inaccurate and unjust. What statistics do show is that among men and women living openly homosexual lives, drunkenness is far more common among lesbians than among male homosexuals. And along with the drunkenness go fights, brawls and suicide attempts commoner among the women than among the men.

It would be unjust and inaccurate of me, however, to leave

the impression that all women homosexuals drink, fight, quarrel and make suicide attempts. On the positive side they show more constancy in their partnerships than men do. While affection and eroticism both play a part in male as in female homosexuality, affection, tenderness and fidelity seem more important among women than among men.

Yet the fact remains that the gay world is far from as gay as its name. As your age advances your chances of loneliness increase. Young faces are fair, young bodies beautiful, young movements quick and eager. But who is attracted by a "tired, old fairy"? Aging people in Western society know how it feels to spend hours in solitude and to sense the impatience and snubs of younger people. They feel the dreariness of enforced idleness and the stigma of uselessness. But at least they are entitled to some respect. They may still have a place of their own and the love of their families. How much emptier is the prospect of the elderly homosexual, living in a gray nether world that only his kind inhabit. Who cares for him? Who wants him around?

Can Homosexuals Be "Cured"?

The question of whether or not homosexuals can be cured in its turn raises more questions. Can you "cure" something which is not a sickness? Is homosexuality a sickness? Homosexuals do not think so. And neither do I.

You will remember that I began this chapter by emphasizing that homosexuality is something you practice rather than something you are. The real question then is, Can homosexual habits be changed? Can new sexual patterns be developed? For homosexual habits are the results of homosexual cravings, cravings that torture the bodies and minds of their enslaved victims. Can the cravings themselves be taken away?

Much depends on what the homosexual wants. Does he or she want to change? Most homosexuals do not. Many resent the attitude of orthodox psychiatry more bitterly even than they resent the attitudes of Christians. What right have psychiatrists to call them sick, much less to try to cure them? Sin is something you can flaunt in the preacher's face, but sickness is too close to craziness to flaunt at anyone. Other homosexuals are too depressed to care what anyone thinks. The possibility of change to another way of life seems too fraught with pain, too costly, too remote to appeal to them.

One middle-aged homosexual who visited me in my office even raised my suspicions as to whether he wanted me to change him or whether he hoped to change me.

"I'm a fruit," he said. "What can you do for me?" His handsome tanned face broadened into a warm grin as he looked me full in the eye. He eased himself comfortably into the chair looking at me all the time. Casually he discussed his preferred techniques, the kind of partners he enjoyed. Teasingly he would break down any attempt on my part to be straightforward or professional. Did I really know what the life was like? Gradually it dawned on me that I was being propositioned. Once I showed no interest in his oblique invitation, he showed none in my proffered help and never came back again.

What does psychiatry offer the homosexual? Psychoanalysis hopes to help him by slowly enabling him to gain insight into his passivity and his fear of women, and their roots in his past relationship with his mother. It hopes that the insight gained will set him free. In spite of occasional success stories, there is no statistical evidence that psychoanalysis has much to offer homosexuals. Moreover the "treatment" is long and extremely expensive.

Other forms of treatment, behavioral and otherwise, aim to force the homosexual to face the thing he fears: female sexuality and sexual relations with females. In doing so they raise, at times, serious moral questions for the Christian.

I remember a flash of rage in my clinical supervisor's eyes when I raised the point. I was a psychiatric resident at the time. My supervisor, a skillful therapist, had been successful in teaching young homosexual males how to conduct a courtship with girl friends of their choice to the point of successful sexual relations with them. His technique was fairly directive (that is, he would make positive suggestions to his patients as well as interpretations of their behavior). Thus he would give them moral support and ideas in dating, in handholding, and in coping with their anxieties and fears as they began their first tentative attempts to enter into a personal relationship and then a more intimate one with a girl.

To be perfectly fair my clinical supervisor was not just skillful. He was a man of integrity and sympathy. He did not do what he did because he got a vicarious kick out of teaching young men to seduce girls. His empathy with the fears and pain of his clients was real.

To him my moral scruples were selfish. Because of them I was denying young homosexuals a normal and happy life. Yet I sensed his anger arose from a doubt in his own mind. Whichever of us was right, I seemed to have touched a raw nerve in his conscience.

Yet if a young homosexual can be guided into heterosexual patterns of behavior by being taught how to engage in sexual foreplay and even sexual relations with a willing partner, are we not justified in helping him to overcome his homosexuality in this way? Will not the end justify the means? Certainly if such a procedure may spell the eventual difference between a normal married life for the young man and the lonely miseries of the gay world, should it at least not be considered? But what guarantee do we have that it will work?

I have already made the Bible's teaching on premarital sex clear. The question, Shall we do evil that good may come? has only one answer for the Christian.

But other, practical questions plague me. The most we can say for my former supervisor's technique is that it opened the way to normal sexual behavior. What guarantee do we have that it closed the door to homosexual behavior? The two are not the same. Many homosexuals enjoy sex with women. Again, are there alternate ways of accomplishing the same, if limited result, without resorting to premarital sex?

Innumerable gadgets and techniques rooted in learning theory are currently being used to teach homosexual patients the same thing. All are based on reinforcement, reward and punishment principles.

Let us say Jim takes the cure. First he will be taught to relax. He might even be given some form of electrical or quick-acting chemical relaxation to take away his anxiety. He will then, in a darkened room, be shown a series of pictures of three basic types. Some slides Jim looks at will be "neutral" (landscapes, pleasant scenes and so on). Others will be "heterosexual" slides and yet others "homosexual." The sexual slides will be graded carefully.

For instance Jim might find himself looking at one of a normal girl to start off with. Little by little, however, the pictures will become more explicitly sexual. The girls will steadily look more like pinups. Jim will also find himself looking at pictures of sex play between men and women, and eventually at extremely erotic and explicit photographs of sexual intercourse. In the same way there will be a gradation in the homosexual pictures he sees.

And Jim will not enjoy the process. At times he will experience anxiety, fear and even panic. He does not derive the same erotic kicks from pornography that many other men would, though the homosexual pictures will be pleasant and sexually arousing to him.

The object of the treatment is to extinguish the pleasurable feelings he gets from the homosexual pictures, while removing the anxiety, fear and panicky excitement aroused by the heterosexual pictures. The hope is that the learning carried out in the sessions will generalize so that Jim's whole feelings about sex will change from homosexual to heterosexual. Men will begin to turn him off, and girls will begin to turn him on.

As each slide is shown Jim will be battered simultaneously by a second set of stimuli. As he watches a neutral scene he will be relaxed—electrically or chemically or by voluntarily relaxing his muscles. The process may be helped by his listening to soothing music. He will feel good watching the picture. At first only mildly heterosexual pictures will be shown and again relaxing techniques will allay his fears and panic. But when homosexual slides are thrown in with the others, immediately Jim will be startled by harsh, loud noises, electric shocks and other unpleasant sensations. Before long he will begin to dread homosexual pictures. At the same time he will experience growing confidence and peace as he is faced with explicitly heterosexual scenes.

Unquestionably such treatments can produce profound changes in homosexuals. A lot depends on how much Jim wishes to change. Some men who take the course are too badly shaken to go on. It is all too frightening. They are not able to take it and so give up part way through.

The weakness in the treatment programs is that their effects are temporary. Follow-up studies show they wear off unless the subjects allow their changed feelings to affect their real-life behavior. Jim must not only go through the mill of the sessions. He must also avoid homosexual temptation and pursue relationships with women to get the full benefit from treatment.

For Jim, personally, this might raise a few practical problems though no moral ones. The Christian homosexual on the other hand faces both. First, the treatment itself involves what he would regard as pornography. Second, how can one benefit from and reinforce the treatment if to do so involves practicing premarital sex? We have already looked at the second question, and I will not go over the ground again.

The pornography does not worry me. I may be wrong (I shall discuss pornography later), but it seems to me that the evil in an explicitly sexual picture does not lie in its sexuality but in the motive that produced it and the use to which it is put. If it is used as a substitute for real sex, the least we can say is that it is in poor taste and that it cheapens sex. But in treatments I have described the pictures are a way of reducing fear about sex. I may be wrong but I see only good in this. *If sex were in itself evil and dirty, it would be a different matter.* What is portrayed in the pictures is not necessarily evil (a lot depends on whom and what is portrayed). But explicitly sexual pictures are not in themselves evil. Only insofar as they are designed to promote promiscuity do they become so.

One of many methods of treating homosexuality involves what is called posthypnotic suggestion. Let us say Joe is ashamed of his homosexual habits, is attracted by a girl and wants to overcome his homosexual feelings. The therapist puts him into a hypnotic trance and feeds his mind new ideas while it is in a condition peculiarly open to them. Joe might be told, for instance, to make a fist. He will then be told that his fist symbolizes his manhood. The tighter it clenches, the more of a real man he is becoming. At the same time he will be told that he is becoming increasingly confident and that women will be attracted by his manliness.

Follow-up studies on homosexuals who have undergone such treatment are interesting. Some homosexuals are dramatically changed. Many are not helped at all. The changes seem to have little to do with motivation (the therapist's guess as to how desperately Joe wanted to change). Nor do they seem to depend either on how deeply ingrained the homosexual habits were or on the skill of the hypnotist. The key factor seems to be the depth of the hypnosis.

For hypnosis, as most people know, is a strange, little understood trance state with varying depths. You can be lightly hypnotized or very deeply hypnotized. Occasionally stage hypnotists have got into difficulties by getting someone so deep that they cannot get them to wake up again.

Hypnosis bothers many Christians. To some it is evil and demonic. There seems to be something supernatural about the power the hypnotist is exercising.

Their fears have some foundation in fact, but mostly they arise from ignorance. Hypnotists have no power. The hypnotist cannot "make" Joe do anything Joe does not really want to do. Joe is not under a spell. The trance state is self-induced. All that has happened is that Joe has voluntarily, under the hypnotist's instructions, relinquished his normal judgment and power to assess reality. He is able to accept any instructions or ideas that are put to him provided he really wants to do so and provided the instructions lie within his physical potential. The hypnotist cannot put one over on Joe or the trance state would immediately break. Dramatic stage demonstrations are possible only because the hypnotized people have unconscious wishes either to do the things they are told to do or else to be the center of the audience's attention. Stage hypnotists do not give anyone supernatural strength. They only make use of the latent strength all of us already have.

Demonic danger in hypnosis is no different from demonic danger in many other spheres. If I wish to open my mind to demonic or sinful control under hypnosis, I may do so. But demons and sin are not particular. They will accept my invitation whether I am under hypnosis or not.

The real moral issue has to do with truth. Is the hypnotist implanting lies into Joe's mind when he is telling him he is becoming more of a man? Is he making him believe something that is fundamentally untrue?

I do not understand how posthypnotic suggestion works. It is not miraculous. It has nothing to do with the supernatural. And it cannot turn a lie into the truth. What seems to happen to Joe is that under hypnosis he can be stripped of the false fears he had of sexuality and given confidence in the manhood he really does possess. He is able to relinquish a lie about himself—even a lie he profoundly believed in (the lie that he did not possess a man's nature)—and accept the truth. By the same token Joe could also allow himself to believe a lie he really wanted to believe. It is Joe's belief system that changes, at a very profound level.

But I must beware of giving an exaggerated view of the usefulness of hypnosis. It is only the exceptional homosexual, the one who not only wants to be cured, but who is able to enter a deep trance, who seems to be helped in this way. And as in all forms of cure, it must be followed up by real-life experiences if it is to produce permanent changes.

There are many other techniques to help homosexuals, but I feel that I have already devoted enough time to the subject. It is better that we proceed to deal with other issues that arise.

How Should Christians View Homosexuality?

When I learned of the monthly gay banquet attended by hundreds of gay men and women in my home city, my spirit was crushed and my heart bowed low in prayer. I felt no anger. Only a yearning possessed me, a yearning that cried to God over the misery of people who call themselves gay. I know some of them personally. I know their heartaches, their angers, their jealousies, their loneliness, their miseries and their pain. I also know God loves them.

Paul uses strong language about sexual perversion in Romans 1, but there are reasons for this which I shall deal with later. What bothers me now is the horror with which so many Christians recoil from homosexuals. Men seem to recoil more than women. Curiously enough, male Christians usually have little feeling, if any, about female homosexuality. It merely puzzles them. But toward their fellow men who are homosexual their attitude is too often one of disgust, contempt and self-righteous superiority. How they thank God that they are not as homosexuals are!

Have you ever paused to think what kind of a quandary this puts the Christian homosexual into? To whom can he turn for help if he wants it? Where can he go for the warmth and understanding he yearns for? The straights either despise him or are embarrassed by his approach. The gays open their arms wide to him. If the non-Christian homosexual faces a social dilemma, the Christian homosexual's dilemma is far more difficult.

Homosexual acts are sinful acts. There may be reasons for them. But reasons only explain, they do not excuse. My sym-

pathy for homosexuals does not amount to approval of homosexuality.

But I must elaborate on this. There is little teaching in the
Bible on homosexuality. We presume it was common in
Sodom, but we are nowhere told that fire fell on Sodom because of its homosexuality. The judgment came down on a
community of many wickednesses of which homosexuality
was but one.

Homosexuality is mentioned only seven times in the Bible,
and then but briefly (Gen. 19:1-11; Lev. 18:22; 20:13; Judg.
19:22-25; Rom. 1:25-26; 1 Cor. 6:9; 1 Tim. 1:9-10). In none
of them is homosexuality approved. In several of them it is
suggested that the practice is not only sinful but unnatural or
perverted. In Leviticus it is made subject to the death penalty.
But in Leviticus as in the Pauline letters it is not singled out as
being worse than a number of other sins, both sexual and non-
sexual all of which (in the Old Testament) called for capital
punishment and all of which (in the New Testament) are seen
as totally incompatible with new life in Christ. We must then
beware of singling out this one sin as being above all others to
be condemned. Scripture does not teach this.

Moreover it is not the sin itself which seems to awaken the
wrath of God or of men of God in the Old and New Testa-
ments. Rather it is the defiant attitude of glorying in their
shame (an attitude which characterizes many homosexuals)
which calls forth divine indignation. The laughing demands
of the lusters of Sodom and of the men in Judges 19 find their
parallels in the Greco-Roman civilization of Paul's day and in
the gay movement leaders of today. It is this defiance of the
divine order which is so offensive.

Let us then have done with a blanket condemnation of and
scorn for homosexuals. No two homosexuals are the same.
Certainly their attitudes toward their behavior vary, as we
have seen already. Many Christian homosexuals, still in bondage to their habit, bitterly long to be free.

But if the homosexual wants to be free, what is to stop him?

Why does he not simply "claim victory by faith"?

So easy to say, isn't it! Are you free from sin, you who "cannot understand" homosexuals? No, you say, "But I don't do *that* sort of thing." Perhaps not. But there are areas of sin in your life that the homosexual could point to, areas in which he has no problem at all.

So far as the problem of "victory" is concerned, we are back where we were in the chapter on masturbation. The big difference is that homosexuality is truly an interpersonal relationship. It involves another person. Masturbation does not. And we must look at the interpersonal aspect of homosexuality a little more before we discuss how a Christian homosexual can come to grips with his sin.

Throughout this book I have emphasized that God gave us sex to teach us communion, to end our aloneness. Sexual love is a model by means of which we can learn a higher type of loving communion, the loving communion between Christ and his church. Homosexuals are deeply aware of the relation between physical sex and the ending of loneliness, as we have already seen.

In the perfectly ordered world of God's creation, everything has its exact place and function. Any deviation from the pattern not only violates his will but frustrates the purpose behind that will.

Now sexual love is also creative love. As our children are born, new stresses are placed upon the love and the companionship of the young parents. They are stresses which will take the marriage in one of two directions. Either the advent of children will erode and even destroy the closeness of the parents, or else, not only because of the newly shared joys but by means of the newly shared pains and stresses, bring about a breadth as well as a depth of communion that neither had ever before dreamed possible. Children may destroy a marriage or deepen and widen the sharingness beyond understanding.

This was what God intended. What happens in practice is

often, tragically, quite different. Divine possibilities are constantly being missed because of sin.

But where, in a homosexual relationship is there room for such a development? It does not exist. It does not exist because the homosexual relationship was never intended to be. And if the explanation I give above is not enough, does not common sense tell us that a vagina was not really designed by God for fingers, tongues or candelsticks? What can *they* do to fertilize an ovum? Nor were mouths or rectal cavities designed to accomodate a penis. A mouth was designed to bite, to chew and to masticate. A rectum was designed to expel feces.

Now having said all this let us make no mistake as to what the Bible condemns. Nowhere is a man or woman condemned for having homosexual feelings. *It is the act, not the urge, that is condemned.* Let us lay aside, for the time being, the question of whether a homosexual can be delivered from all homosexual feelings and desires. Let us assume that many never will be.

In that case a homosexual is in exactly the same position as a straight person whose circumstances demand chastity. Peter, an unmarried twenty-three-year-old teacher may feel very strong sexual urges. Provided he does not go out of his way to get turned on, no one may condemn him for this. His urges are the product of God-given instincts and the stimulation he cannot avoid in the world we live in. So, Peter, do not feel guilty that you find yourself tormented. It is unpleasant, but it is not wicked. What you must not do is practice fornication. Flee temptation. It is one thing to feel the urge. It is quite another to allow it to take over.

In the same way I must continue to insist that while God condemns homosexual acts, he nowhere condemns homosexual feelings. Many Christian men and women who have struggled with homosexuality are courageously facing lives of comparative loneliness and complete chastity. They hold my deepest admiration. They have recognized their problem, committed to God their special vulnerabilities and make-up, and are prepared to face life *as they are* until he should see fit to deliver them. And like Shadrach, Meshach and Abednego their attitude is that whether God shall intervene to deliver them or not, they will not, by God's grace, break their vow of chastity. They will live lives of sexual abstinence. I praise God from the bottom of my heart for such soldiers of the cross. They are indeed eunuchs for the kingdom of heaven's sake.

What about Friendship?

It would be wise to add here a word about friendships. The word *homosexual* is too often a term of abuse. For some men and women marriage has no appeal. They find their friendships and companionships among members of their own sex. The friendship in question may grow so deep that we may truly speak of love between them.

How are we to view such love? Are we to curl our lips and call it homosexual? There may be no erotic relationship involved at all. Are we to say that the friendship (even the living together) is somehow unclean, perverted? Do we say that the absence of physical sex makes no difference, that it really is a homosexual relationship?

How about David and Jonathan? Between the two of them there was a love "passing the love of women" (2 Sam. 1:26). Was the affection between them basically sexual?

C. S. Lewis has some wise words to say about friendship in his book *The Four Loves*. He speaks of friends as being "shoulder to shoulder" rather than (as lovers) "face to face." Among the many things he points out is that friends welcome a third of like mind to their number.

Friendship is God's gift to the man or woman who is not able to marry. Let me quote Lewis.

Friendship arises out of mere companionship when two or more companions discover that they have in common some insight or interest or even taste which the others do not share and which, till that moment, each believe to be his own unique treasure (or burden). The typical expression of opening friendship would be something like "What? You too? I thought I was the only one". . . .

Lovers *seek for* privacy. Friends find solitude about them,
this barrier between them and the herd, *whether they want it
or not.* They would be glad to reduce it. The first two would
be glad to find a third.[6] (My emphasis.)

There exists, therefore, a love we call friendship which is
fundamentally different from erotic love. Both are gifts from
God. Both are given to ease our aloneness. Both reflect one
aspect of God's relationship with us. But they are not to be
confused. They are not the same thing.

If you are someone who has been denied erotic love, then
be grateful if God should give you friendship-love for others
of your own sex. Ignore raised eyebrows. If people believe
something exists between you and your friend that does not,
do not try to prove them wrong. People sometimes believe in
invisible canaries, and it is very difficult to prove to someone
who wants to believe in them that invisible canaries do not
exist.

But we must make one more point clear. Erotic love and
friendship love *can* coincide. In a good marriage they always
do. In a homosexual relationship they also may. Where erotic
feelings arise in a friendship or where jealousy begins to
poison it, it is better to face the fact that the friendship-love
may include elements of erotic love. But for every friendship
where erotic and friendship-love coexist, there are hundreds
of thousands of God-given friendship-loves with no trace of
eros—except in the unclean minds of the envious observers
from outside.

What Should Christian Homosexuals Do?

Christian homosexuals should not practice homosexuality.

No psychiatric help or "cure" is needed to quit the practice.
Go to a trustworthy friend, perhaps a Christian counselor or
prayer partner with whom you can be perfectly open and
frank. Make a clean breast of your story. Talk with him. Pray
with him. But so far as your practice of homosexuality is con-

cerned *it must stop. Now.* And if it has not yet started, then it must never be allowed to.

I know what pain this might cause you. Straight friends may find it hard to understand that you may deeply love someone of your own sex and that to break up with your lover will wound you in the same way as the breakup of any kind of illicit love wounds those involved. I know too that a period of sadness and even of profound depression may follow the breakup.

But do not fool yourself. You *can* do it. And you must. Whatever God may or may not do for you in the way of changing your sexual orientation, he can and will deliver you from any specific homosexual entanglement and from all homosexual activity.

Your part is simply to quit. He does not promise freedom from grief or pain. But he does promise strength and consolation.

Flee temptation. Avoid the company of anyone who specially turns you on. Avoid places and circumstances which expose you to sexual arousal. This may cramp your lifestyle, but the price you pay is a bargain price for what you gain in fellowship with God.

As for the feelings and tendencies, these are another matter. I have described some ways in which psychologists and psychiatrists attempt to change homosexual feelings and urges. Their success is real but limited. And as we have seen the methods raise a number of moral problems—not the least of which is, Should a Christian seek such help at all? Should he or she not rather look to God to change them in answer to believing prayer? Should a Christian, for example, act in faith and seek to marry, trusting God to change his or her orientation?

These questions affect a wider group of people than practicing homosexuals. Many single men and women as well as some married ones experience homosexual feelings. Most closely conceal their secret urges even from themselves, fearful that they may discover they are abnormal (and tragically, their fears are sometimes groundless).

Marriage and the Homosexual
Let us be clear about one thing. Marriage in and of itself, never "cures" homosexuality. Experience has shown that it may even deepen the frustration of the homosexual partners and bewilder and humiliate the ones they marry.

This is not to say that marriage should not be contemplated, only that it must be considered very seriously and carefully, and with a full awareness of the problems it may involve. It should never be contemplated as an easy escape from homosexual feelings.

The biggest problem is not one of sexual arousal (or the absence of it) between the partners. Sexual arousal and enjoyable sexual relations can be learned under skilled counseling and help. The greatest problems are emotional ones and call for clear and full communication between the partners. What does each expect of the other in marriage? How easy is it for each to *give* understanding, and how does the capacity to give compare in each partner with the need to *receive* understanding? If both partners need to be loved more than they are able to *give* love, the marriage, like any marriage is headed for trouble.

How fully has the problem of homosexuality been shared; and how easy is it for both to discuss it? Has the homosexual partner unconsciously picked a partner like his parent of the opposite sex? To do so is fine if the relationship with both parents was a good one. It can lead to trouble otherwise.

Both marriage partners should spend time with a wise and experienced counselor in whom they can confide. Moreover they should do so before their friendship has gone so far that to break it off is painful and difficult.

Life for the Homosexual
I must revert to two questions before concluding this chapter.

The first one is, Should a homosexual seek to be made straight in his feelings and sexual orientation? And if so how? By divine intervention or by psychological means? The second question is, What about homosexuals who feel sure that their nature will not change or who do not wish it to change? What does life hold for them? What does God have for them in life?

Let me deal with the first question, the question of using natural means to make a homosexual straight. *There is no conflict between believing God and taking treatment.* To insist that it must be either God or psychology is to put God in a box.

Let us make one thing clear. Faith must always be in God, never in man. There is only one real Source of healing and help, and from that Source all healing comes. The question is not whether we choose God or psychology. The choice lies between God's direct, miraculous intervention and his more ordinary working. For psychiatrists and psychologists can only offer help in so far as they have (wittingly or unwittingly) stumbled across God's laws and applied them wisely.

Man is God's creation. Man's personality develops and changes for better or worse in accordance with divine laws. Those who study those laws (even though they may not always know the Creator of them) can give real help by using them.

God is able to intervene miraculously, but he has nowhere promised to do so every time we wish it. "Ask and ye shall receive" was not given as a credit card to buy any kind of merchandise. To demand that God shall accede to our wishes whatever they be and whenever we wish is to treat God as magicians treat the powers of darkness. It is only as we ask according to his will that he hears us. And while it is clearly his will that we never engage in homosexuality, it is by no means clear that it is his will to change our sexual orientation immediately. He may have (as we discussed in the chapter on masturbation) a prior series of works to perform in our lives, operations that are from his point of view of greater importance. And even if such should not be the case, God does not always choose to work miraculously when natural means of help are close at hand. To pray, "Give us this day our daily bread," does not excuse us from work. To pray, "Satisfy my thirst, Lord," does not absolve us from the responsibility of turning on a faucet.

Therefore if you desire to experience a change in your sexual feelings, pray about what God would have you do. Find out what help is available in your area, and what the treatment involves. If you have doubts about moral and ethical points, discuss the matter with a Christian counselor or a Christian doctor whose judgment you can trust.

You may find there is a road to a normal sexual life for you. But on the other hand you may not.

Life as a "Nonheterosexual"

But what has life to offer you if marriage and normal sexual relations will never be yours? Do you see it as a bleak, endless stretch of days, months, years? Of frustrated longing? Of bitter loneliness?

I am not sure that we have begun with the right question. But now we have asked it, How about it? What does life have to offer you?

Yet are we asking? Are we implying by our question that you are worse off than other people? If so we must stop right here. You *are* worse off—*in one way.* So is a blind man or a deaf man. Helen Keller was both blind and deaf (yet she enriched the lives of millions).

It will not help you to see yourself as *more unfortunate than everyone else.* You have a personal tragedy. So have many people. *Their* tragedies may seem trivial to you. (Grass is always greener in other pastures.) But to each one his tragedy can be an unbearable burden or a source of strength. If you want to spend the rest of your life feeling bitter and sorry for yourself, you will have only yourself to blame for your suffering. "Two men looked out of prison bars. The one saw mud; the other, stars."

What does life offer you?

For one thing it offers you a High Priest who understands you perfectly. "Therefore he [Christ] had to be made like his brethren," the writer of Hebrews tells us, *"in every respect....* For because he himself has suffered and been tempted, he is able to help those who are tempted.... For we have not a high priest who is unable to sympathize with our weaknesses, but one who in every respect has been tempted as we are, yet without sin" (Heb. 2:17-18; 4:15).

In *every* respect? In *all* ways? What is it saying? Tempted to lie? To steal? To commit adultery? I tremble to let my thoughts venture further. Yet as I check the words and the various translations I cannot avoid their meaning. Our thoughts recoil at what they could mean. Tempted in a homosexual way? Jesus? God the Son? Is this blasphemy ... or is it at the very core of the gospel message? How could he represent sinners whose sins he had never faced and conquered? Can you see now why I insist that it is the homosexual *act* not the homosexual *temptation* God condemns. For Jesus was tempted *yet without sin.*

I have no wish to dwell upon the point, for my head bows in shame. Yet at the same time it bows in wonder, in awe and in reverence. Before he could be my representative and substitute, he must have faced all that I have faced—and faced it to the full. He was the perfect offering because he had been made perfect in the very fierceness and foulness of the temptations he endured. He was no alabaster statue. He was no painting with soulful eyes. He was the Son of man.

So now he can "sympathize with our weaknesses." He can do more than cleanse. He can understand. He can plead with God. There is a High Priest for the homosexual who can understand the homosexual because he knows from personal experience what homosexual temptation feels like.

"Oh yes," you say, "but he must have brushed it aside before ever he felt it!" It would be nice to think that, wouldn't it? And I have no doubt about the speed with which Jesus would brush *all* temptation aside. I have no question about this.

137

Yet all that is beside the point. Temptation comes from a tempter, a tempter who is skilled at playing on human physiology. Jesus faced that tempter *as a man*. And the tempter may have departed for a season from time to time, but his attacks were fierce and persistent and unrelenting. So Jesus can understand all about temptation of any and every variety. Praise God and kneel in adoration!

What is there in life for the nonheterosexual? There is still human friendship. Not all friendship need arouse sexual temptation. Ask God to give you friends, close friends. To be sure, you must give friendship if you are to receive it. But pray for friends and seek them.

Loneliness? You may have lots. Yet as John Donne pointed out two centuries ago, loneliness is God's great opportunity to draw near the soul.[7] Would you despise intimacy with the Almighty in insisting on more of human intimacy?

I began this section by suggesting we had asked the wrong question. Viktor Frankl, the Viennese psychoanalyst, would put it this way. "Is the question," he would ask us, "what we expect of life? Or is it rather what life expects of us?"[8]

There is something to life that only a Christian homosexual can offer. A moment ago we discussed the wonder of our High Priest's understanding of our weaknesses. For the man or woman who discovers it, this can be comfort beyond measure. But it is comfort to be passed on. "The Father of mercies and God of all comfort," Paul writes, "who comforts us in all our affliction, so that we may be able to comfort those who are in any affliction, with the comfort with which we ourselves are comforted by God" (2 Cor. 1:3-4).

"In any affliction? In the pressure of homosexual temptation?"

Yes, "by the comfort which we ourselves are comforted by God."

"But would it not be just as good if all my homosexual feelings ended? I could still help them from past experience."

Unfortunately it does not always work like that. The apostle goes on, "For as we share abundantly in Christ's sufferings, so through Christ we share abundantly in comfort too" (2 Cor. 1:5).

The sufferings of Christ are those sufferings we endure by reason of our faithfulness to him. If you are a nonheterosexual who lives a chaste life because of your faithfulness to Christ, you will inevitably suffer. Your sufferings will in this case be "the sufferings of Christ" every bit as much as any other sufferings that spring from following Christ. Those sufferings may abound. They may be great and tumultuous. But their greatness will be compensated by a greater consolation, and their tumult by a greater, "Peace, be still!"

I do not know the specific thing the world and the kingdom of God expect of you. But I know it will be a unique thing that you alone can offer; I know that it will arise from abundant suffering.

And I know also that it will spring from a superabundant glory of consoling peace.

7
DEEDS DONE IN THE DARK

There are pitiful things that lonely people, particularly lonely men, do in their shameful extremities. Old men approach little girls in dark streets. Young men may stand at their window at night with their genitals exposed and shine a flashlight on themselves when girls walk by. Peeping Toms, from thirteen years old to seventy years old haunt streets or apartment blocks on a rare chance of experiencing vicarious sex by sneaking a glance through an uncurtained window.

I have known men to slither up the slippery surfaces of snow covered garage roofs, risking both discovery and a broken neck, just on the off chance of seeing something titillating through a crack in a partly closed bedroom curtain above the garage roof. I have known men to haunt high-rise apartment buildings, stalking carpeted corridors, dropping to their knees before a mail box and peering in. Some apartments, you see, have mail box openings that give a full view of a settee in the living room. And from seven to nine in the evening in certain apartments, couples are having sex on the settee in one out of every fifteen to twenty apartments. The ratio is higher in summer if the apartment has a swimming pool.

But the stalker has to be on his guard. If he hears the opening of elevator doors further down the corridor, he must be off his knees—and quickly.

And what does he have after an hour of sneaking around? *Perhaps* one glimpse of lovemaking plus a lot of anxiety, a feeling of self-contempt, of emptiness and of being an alien in a world where everyone else seems to be sexually fulfilled. He drives home feeling like a little boy in an adult world and hides his face when his wife greets him with a smile. He is not the monster of horror fiction at all. But in time his conscience may become seared and scarred.

There are also people, whether they read the Marquis de Sade or not, who get their thrills by inflicting or receiving pain and others by dressing in the clothes of the opposite sex. Some are sexually aroused by a glove, by a shoe, by a piece of underwear. Ask them why and they cannot tell you though often they are ashamed.

Some fathers teach their daughters about sex in a cozy little interview with a father-daughter demonstration. Some daughters are terror-stricken, besides being oppressed by terrible guilt when their sexual feelings are aroused. Others like it. They have told me so. They have also told me they know how to turn dad on and to beat mother at the game. And these things happen *in Christian families*.

Mothers, too, take their young sons to bed. It begins innocently—or at least unconsciously. But it develops to a lover relationship.

Still others have sex with animals, or even, rarely, with the dead.

A Sullied Masterpiece

We have words for these and other perversions: exhibitionism, voyeurism, fetishism, pedophilia, sadism, masochism, incest, sodomy, necrophilia. We also have theories about them and various forms of treatment for them.

For me to pursue the details of them further would be either to turn this chapter into a clinical textbook or else into an unsavoury chapter for vicarious voyeurism. Already I have said quite enough.

Why have I mentioned these things at all?

First, I want all Christians to understand that the vast majority of people I have mentioned are not dangerous. A few, a very few, are. The majority are unhappy, inadequate and lonely. Something has gone wrong that causes them to be excited in a way that makes them take stupid risks (sometimes the risk is part of the thrill) only to find that it was not worth it and that they despise themselves in deepening depression for doing what they do and for being what they are. Fathers who seduce their daughters are often inadequate as men. Voyeurs arouse my sympathy the most. They make me think of small dogs with their tails between their legs. I long to coax them to lift their heads up again.

My second purpose is to speak a word of comfort to people who conceal the shame of the strange enslavements in which they are bound. You may already have discovered, you who have an off-beat hang-up, that discovery and punishment, however painful and embarrassing, did nothing to help you. I know a voyeur who has been beaten up twice, has served a jail sentence, and faces the loss of his job. Yet none of these things stopped his peeping.

I do not know you, of course, but if you are like many people I know, somewhere near the root of your habit lies a lack of respect for yourself. When no one is watching you, when you are alone and quiet, is it not true that you sometimes feel certain that you are no good? That you (not just your behavior but *you yourself*) are despicable? Many men and women with bizarre sexual hang-ups have told me this is how they feel. And nothing is more demoralizing, nothing more destructive of hope than secretly to hate, despise or despair of oneself.

You are not despicable. You were made in the image of God. That image in you may have been defaced, yet still it is there. And a defaced masterpiece is better far than the unspoiled statue of a third-rate artist. You are a sullied masterpiece. Behind the ugliness and sin you are of more innate worth than the whole universe of stars and suns.

But you will never feel this way about yourself until you take the risk of exposing your inner self—of revealing what you are ashamed of—to someone else. I use the word risk with care. I cannot guarantee that you will not encounter rejection and further humiliation. Perhaps you have tried to follow my suggestion and already been disappointed. Yet try again you must.

There are people who will not despise you whatever your hang-up may be. What you need is to warm your soul in the sunshine of another person's respect and understanding and in so doing begin to rediscover respect for yourself. If your problem is not too deeply ingrained, this of itself may be enough to begin to set you free.

Your soul may be warmed yet more. There exists a God in heaven to whom I have referred many times in this book. Not only did he make you; he has made provision to make you whole. If you are already a Christian, you are not only doubly precious to him because of the price paid for your redemption, you are beautiful in his eyes. He sees you in Christ.

If you are not a Christian, discovery awaits you. The Jesus who burst out of a tomb came to heal such as you. "Those who are well have no need of a physician, but those who are sick," he once said. "I came not to call the righteous, but sinners." (Mt. 9:12-13). The problem you hide is at the same time a sickness and a sin. From him it draws only compassion and love. Whether he will choose to intervene miraculously and take away the problem itself I cannot say. But he can and does forgive. And he can and will receive you, whatever your hang-up.

You may, however, have given up hope already. You may have no desire to change. It may seem to you that you are too feeble, too offbeat ever to be delivered. You may no longer care.

I wish it were in my power to awaken hope within you. The hang-up you have may be embarrassing, but embarrassing and despicable are not the same. Some people assume that the weirder the behavior the more sinful or sick it is. But this does not necessarily follow. A hole in my sock or a split in the seat of my pants makes me horribly embarrassed. A run in my wife's stockings or having her slip show embarrasses her. It could be that the habit you have is the behavioral equivalent of holes in socks or runs in stockings—something to be concealed if at all possible but not accurately reflecting one's personal worth.

I once knew a man who got a sexual thrill out of his cat. He could hardly talk about the matter, and his wife and daughter had scornfully broadcast his perversion throughout the neighborhood. He was bitter and humiliated. When he discovered that I respected him, his whole body changed. His shoulders had been drooped, his head bowed, while his eyes never met mine. But a transformation took place before my eyes as he straightened his back and looked at me.

I would mislead you if I gave you the impression that hope and self-respect alone will solve your problem. In practice they constitute a good start, but you may also need professional counsel or therapy. It is wise to look for such therapy early. There must be help somewhere at hand. Try your physician. Or look out for a counseling clinic. Talk to a minister of a church. You have nothing to lose and everything to gain. You may get nowhere the first time you try, but do not give up.

A Word to the Church

I have yet a third purpose in mentioning what is so rarely mentioned in Christian books (except the Bible). I want to defend the victims I have been addressing, to defend them from the Christian public. Such people need Christian forgiveness, acceptance, compassion *and* professional help. We must insist that they get the latter and we must do all in our power to see they get a Christian friend, with whom they can come clean and with whom they can pray, who can be their trusted entrée into Christian society. For such men and women, more than any of us, need both the discipline and the support of the church. They need around them people who know them and love them.

Christians tend to react altogether inappropriately when they encounter bizarre sexual sin. Their reaction is not to the gravity of the sin. Rather it is that they fear what they cannot understand. To such Christians I say: Look at the person not at the hang-up. Look at the person through the eyes of Christ and not through the filter of sexual behavior that frightens you. The man or woman before you is not a leper. And even if he were, Christ would have you reach out and touch him. This is what Christian love is all about.

Love, real love, is what above everything else they need. For when the physical bridge God gave man for the building of sexual love has been so weirdly and cruelly distorted, only a consistent and powerful experience of the agape love of Christ, mediated through his people can keep them walking in righteousness.

Is there a church on earth through whom the Spirit can minister such discipline, such acceptance, such love? Is there a church that cares? Or in our pursuit of superorganizations are we building human structures over the bodies and souls of the human tragedies I have been describing? It is in the next chapter that I discuss such questions.

PART III

THE CHURCH & SEXUAL SIN

8
THE
DISCIPLINE
THAT
HEALS

Perhaps churches sometimes do it right. Perhaps the churches' wise and right actions, because the actions are wise and right, attract little attention. But the sex scandals we do hear about are botched and botched stupendously. Let me cite a couple of examples. Each of them is disguised so you will not identify the real characters.

A Tale of Two Churches
Mary was a timid mother of one child, her daughter Cathy. Cathy, like Andrew, her salesman father, was a vivacious extrovert. This troubled Mary because she herself felt so colorless beside her ebullient Andrew and her scintillating Cathy. She blamed her timidity on the great shame of her life: She was an illegitimate child, born of an unknown father to an eighteen-year-old mother ("Who became very respectable

afterwards—at least so the agency told me. They wouldn't tell me her name, but they said she was a nice girl of a very good family"). If you talked for any length of time to Mary, she would quietly confess her secret, watching you with pleading eyes, hoping you would not despise her. All three, Andrew, Mary and Cathy, were members of their local (rural) Baptist church. Andrew was a deacon, Cathy was the president of a teens group and Mary played the piano when the regular pianist was sick.

At thirteen Cathy became pregnant and kept her pregnancy a secret until she was eleven weeks along. Andrew was outraged, taking the matter as a personal affront. His resourcefulness forsook him and his theme song became, "Why, oh why, should it happen to me? Such a good father as I?"

Mary hauled Cathy off to a doctor in the city. To Mary's relief, the doctor recommended a therapeutic abortion at an early date on the grounds of Cathy's age. He obtained the consent of the abortion committee at the local hospital. Cathy was confused. She agreed that she wanted the abortion but spent a number of tearful days as she recovered from it. She dropped out of school temporarily and stayed with an aunt in the city. Mary could think of nothing but the terrible shame of illegitimacy and wept with self-pity at the thought that an illegitimate child had been spared all she had faced herself.

To this day no one knows how the cat got out of the bag, but soon the church was abuzz with rumors. Then came a meeting of the deacons and the minister at Andrew and Mary's home. It was a solemn and uncomfortable meeting. I have only Mary's version to go on and that may not be entirely accurate. The feeling I got was that the deacons had the minister (who was young and inexperienced) on the spot. It almost seemed that the deacons were present in order to see that he did his stuff. Certainly a lot was going on at the meeting that never was expressed in words.

The climax came when one deacon put the question, "Did you or did you not give permission for your daughter to have an abortion?" Mary pressed her lips together. All her timidity dropped from her. "I'm not sure that some of you here are fit persons to be asking such questions," was all she would say. She would admit nothing. Andrew merely protested "I'm saying nothing. I had nothing to do with it."

There were two further meetings. The church, fully aware of what was going on, saw it as a power struggle between the deacons on one side and Andrew and Mary on the other. In actual fact it was a tussle between Mary and the toughest of the deacons. The rest soon had no stomach for the matter and would have dropped it, save that they were all on stage, so to speak, and there was no way out.

In the end Andrew signed some sort of face-saving document in which he stated his regrets for "the incident that had taken place," the incident not being specifically named.

Andrew and Mary are still at the church. Mary longs to leave, but Andrew is reinstated as one of the boys and enjoys his role in the church. Cathy comes home occasionally but avoids the church. She does have active fellowship where she lives now, and though less vivacious than she was, seems to have weathered the storm the best of any of them.

I suppose it would take a long essay to analyze the errors of the sordid little story. To apportion the blame is easy. Everyone was to blame, and in some vague sense our own guilt, the guilt of you who read and I who write, is being laid on the carpet. Who is to say how we would have acted ourselves? Rather than apportion blame we must ask what *should* the church do under similar circumstances? What did they *not* do in the instance above? There are two answers: (1) The church should be able to offer succor and healing to people in sin and in torment; and (2) the church should be able to offer corrective discipline and restore sinners to a place of forgiveness.

You may, on the basis of my first vignette, feel that the big need is succor and counsel; and if so, you would have a number of church fathers and later divines to agree with you. But there are other cases that might point to other conclusions.

Rev. Dr. James D. Melville (not his real name) was an out-standing Bible expositor in a large metropolitan church in the northern United States. He had training in two well-known evangelical seminaries and took extra courses in pastoral counseling. He was a kindly, understanding and an apparently honest man. Domestic trouble became apparent over the years and Mrs. Melville's excessive drinking became an embarrassment to his ministry. The Melvilles consulted the leaders of their church and also took professional counseling. Mrs. Melville went for two periods of institutional treatment.

Over the years her behavior deteriorated and most of their friends regarded her as a hopeless drunk. During this period Dr. Melville's increasingly close association with the church secretary (a divorced woman, converted following her divorce) gave rise to comment. The situation in the church was unhealthy. Dr. Melville announced to the board that he was suing for divorce and offered to resign. He was questioned about his association with the church secretary, agreed that he had been indiscreet, but denied any impropriety on his part.

After a good deal of heated discussion the board, backed by a general meeting of the church membership, expressed its desire for Dr. Melville to continue his ministry, irrespective of his divorce. At this point the church secretary broke down and confessed that she had been having sexual relations with Melville for the previous five years. Melville, badly shaken, admitted that he had been lying in his previous protestations.

The upshot was that Melville, immediately following his divorce, married the former church secretary and was invited by a minority of the members of his old church to be the pastor of a new church they were forming. He accepted their invitation. Slowly, over the past five years, his former church has dwindled to a quarter of its previous membership, and his new church is undertaking a building program to accommodate its greatly expanded congregation.

Help and succor certainly were needed, but the problem of

a church leader who had continued for years in adultery certainly raises the issue of disciplinary action—and disciplinary action of a most perplexing nature, where the offending leader finds acceptance, without discipline, in another church group. Again, what *could* the Holy Spirit be thinking about by blessing Melville's second church? Could Melville not be so bad after all?

Without Resolution or Reconciliation

Before we attempt to look for guidance as to how the church should fulfill her responsibility and what the extent of her responsibility is, we must notice how utterly unsatisfactory were the resolutions of the two incidents I described. In the first incident an official patching-up was negotiated by the leadership of the church. Several different versions of all that had taken place continued to circulate around the community. The gossip lost none of its spice when a document was signed. Mary's heartache doubled. Once a timid, illegitimate woman, she had now become the embittered mother of a daughter she had encouraged to abort. Since she refused to discuss the matter with anyone, she had no idea who thought what of her or her daughter. Her prayers to God were confused and uncertain and nothing in her private devotional life corresponded to anything in her church life.

The young pastor was bewildered and troubled but did not know why. The more he went over matters, the more he could sympathize with everybody else's point of view—which added up to there being no answer at all. He left the ministry after a couple of years with a sense that his call had probably been a mistake. One deacon was entrenched in a position of righteous power, and the others felt he, "was all right, really, and you need a strong man around." Surprisingly, Andrew and the deacon in question got along very well.

Not only is it clear that nothing was really resolved. What also stands out is that the church's responsibilities towards sexual sin cannot be separated from its other failures. Self-will, power-greed, parental failure, man-pleasing, face-saving— all these weaknesses and many more prevented Cathy and her parents from being helped. In this particular instance the Lord Jesus seems to have sent Cathy on her way forgiven while her excusers and accusers formed a new and ill-assorted alliance. It is an alliance *still incompetent to help any other sinner who might come along.*

But we are dealing with negative things. We need to look for positive principles. And one vital need I must mention before we look at any counseling techniques or disciplinary principles is the need for honest, loving courage among God's people. There was no honest, loving courage in Andrew and Mary's church. The pastor (and let us not be hard on him) was anxious to do what would please the deacons. It was his first test. Insecure and uncertain of himself, he wanted to do the right thing. But the "right thing" was the thing that would please the body of men who were praising his sermons and to whom he looked for fatherly support. They were his conscience.

The deacons, on the other hand, had their wives' deep prejudices in place of consciences. In that particular community *abortion* was a bated-breath-wide-eyed-trembling-lips word. After all, what could one expect from an Illegitimate Woman? Blood tells. All the strong elders came home to wives who felt that the terrible thing that had happened could have been predicted years ago. None of the deacons would find it easy. Mighty men in church are sometimes mice at home.

They would sense, too, that the church expected them to "do something." Do what? Put wrong right? Vindicate the church? Put the sinners in their place? They were being scrutinized. This was no private matter. Something was expected of them. Deacons must act like deacons in a crisis of such magnitude. Somehow the situation had arisen in which every man had to justify himself. And you cannot justify yourself to the public and maintain a loving, honest compassion for sinners. He who sees things as God sees them may have to stand alone.

As for Jim Melville, so far as I know no one went to have a brotherly, heart-to-heart talk with him. Some came to tell him that they were standing by him. Others privately said they would like to give him a piece of their mind. Still others declared they would never speak to him again. Many people were scared of him. But to my knowledge no one went and leveled with him in love. There were at least a dozen other godly pastors in the city. I cannot say they lacked love and courage. But they did not go. They did not even call. And now they are all hobnobbing with him like nothing happened. There was for a while the delicate question of his relationship with the Evangelical Pastor's Association, but this seems to have been resolved smoothly.

Nobody really cared enough about Jim Melville, his wife or his secretary. Were they not overtaken in faults? Whose job was it then to restore them "in a spirit of meekness"? Were they being left to bear their own burdens (Gal. 6:1-2)? Everyone seemed more concerned about "my own position" than about somebody else's burden. How did Jim grapple with his guilt? Should he have been discouraged from preaching right away? Did he see the new, little church as an opening from God whereas in fact it made him the pawn of a discontented faction of the church that was hungry for independence and power?

No. Until we are all more concerned for one another as brothers and sisters in Christ, and less concerned with status, reputation, position and church politics, we shall have no hope of responding appropriately to the growing volume of sexual sin in our midst. The sexual sin is a symptom not the disease itself. And while it will help for us to define the church before we delineate her responsibility, it must be apparent to anyone who thinks, that definitions and delineations are academic exercises where concern and godly responsibility are absent.

Three Elements a Church Doth Make

The Reformers differed as to when the church may be said to be truly present. A sentimental evangelical will be satisfied with the verse, "Where two or three are gathered together in my name, there am I in the midst of them" (Mt. 18:20). Where Jesus is, the church is. But the context of the verse makes it clear that a great deal more is involved than a devotional meeting for prayer. A prayer meeting and ecclesia are not the same thing.

For some Reformers like Beza and Alsted the preaching of the pure doctrine of the Word constitute the one exclusive mark of the true church. Their emphasis is understandable. Having seen the appalling effects of wrong teaching in a decadent church, they would naturally be impressed by the need to proclaim the truth. So for them the church existed where the truth was faithfully proclaimed. Many modern evangelicals unconsciously go along with this idea. Yet the truth can be preached ever so powerfully while sin goes rampant and unchecked in the congregation.

For Calvin and others the preaching of the Word was not enough. There had also to be the right administration of the sacraments. These were not to be divorced from the Word of God or even from its visible preaching. Indeed they should only be administered to true believers of the Word and their offspring. There was no magic in the sacraments. They represented simple obedience to Scripture.

But for other Reformers a third element was essential. Acknowledged to be something wholesome, it was for Christians of the Anabaptist tradition an element without which the church did not exist: godly exercise of discipline among its members. In this, at times, they seem to have gone beyond even the Roman Catholic position.

John Howard Yoder feels that the disciplinary passage, Matthew 18:15-20,

> gives more authority to the church than does Rome, trusts more to the Holy Spirit than does pentecostalism, has more

respect for the individual than humanism, makes moral standards more binding than puritanism, is more open to the given situation than the 'new morality.' If practiced, it would change the life of churches more fundamentally than has yet been suggested by the currently popular discussions of changing church structures.[1]

"Where this [church discipline] is lacking, there is certainly no church, even if the Water Baptism and the Supper of Christ are practiced," states Hubmaier.[2]

Let us look at what Jesus taught in this passage:

If your brother sins against you, go and tell him his fault, between you and him alone. If he listens to you, you have gained your brother. But if he does not listen, take one or two others along with you, that every word may be confirmed by the evidence of two or three witnesses. If he refuses to listen to them, tell it to the church; and if he refuses to listen even to the church, let him be to you as even a Gentile and a tax collector. Truly, I say to you, whatever you bind on earth shall be bound in heaven, and whatever you loose on earth shall be loosed in heaven. Again I say to you, if two of you agree on earth about anything they ask, it will be done for them by my Father in heaven. For where two or three are gathered in my name, there am I in the midst of them. (Mt. 18:15-20)

If there is any truth in the assertions of the Anabaptists that the third element of church discipline is required for a true church, we have in the Western world no more than a series of syndicated Christian organizations and clubs, misnamed churches and denominations. They are well organized, well financed, and certainly no one can deny that God the Holy Spirit works through them or that they are a power for good. They even make the occasional token disciplinary gesture. But we may be deceiving ourselves when we call them churches. For certainly any real attempt to regulate the lives of their members is noticeably absent. We cover up. We act with discretion. We are concerned with our public image and our public relations. Our reputation, rather than our testimony, is supremely important to us; so we keep our house reasonably tidy. But the firm, loving discipline of sinning members, so conspicuous in the New Testament, is almost entirely missing. We are the Church of Private People with Private Lives.

At this point I must declare my sympathies with the Anabaptists. However I may differ from them in some matters, however alarmed I may feel about the way some of them practice discipline, I must agree with them that a church without discipline is something less than a church and will never startle a jaded world with its blinding purity any more than with its loving unity.

But the word discipline has unhappy connotations. Was the deacons' meeting in Andrew and Mary's home a form of discipline? Were the ugly rumors, the spiteful comments, the puerile attempts at self-justification essential concommitants of discipline? Is discipline the coalescence of a score of old church resentments around the sinner who got found out? Were the lechers who goaded Jesus about the shame-filled adulteress promoting godly discipline?

Clearly if we must define what we mean by church, we must also describe what we mean by discipline. For discipline cannot be heralded by the cry, "J'accuse!" The communists are very effective in the use of such forms of discipline.

I have come across no more thoughtful and penetrating paper on the disciplinary passage in Matthew 18 than Yoder's study in *Concern*. Modestly described as "a skeleton . . . fragmentary," it deserves to be widely disseminated and studied. Among the points he makes are some we recognize in theory already but also many that shock us.

Jesus talks in the passage about "binding" and "loosing." To us the words seem esoteric and mysterious, linked with heavenly bindings and loosings. Yet from the halakah, the moral tradition of the Jews, and from contemporary Scripture usage, we see that the terms have two dimensions.

To *bind* means to withhold fellowship; to *loose*, to forgive. But there is a secondary meaning, a meaning more commonly understood in the halakah. To bind was to forbid or to command—to declare what was or was not permitted. To loose was to allow, to leave free to choose.

Both sets of meanings are important in Scripture and for a fuller consideration of them I recommend Yoder's study. Yet it is clear at once that if to the church is given powers of withholding fellowship, of declaring forgiveness, of enjoining duties and if heaven backs the church in doing these things, then the church on earth is no mere club or organization. It is a vital extension of heavenly powers of a degree and quality we rarely think about.

Yet it is not my purpose to pursue the awesome implications of Anabaptist doctrine but rather to look at those aspects of discipline on which we may more easily agree and at practical ways of using them to help sexual sinners.

If Your Brother Sins
The words "against you" are absent in many of the older manuscripts.
"If your brother sins, go. . . ." Instantly protests and rationalizations arise in our minds.

"It's not really my business."

"Just what constitutes sin, anyway?"

"I'm hardly qualified, morally, not to mention by training, to interfere."

"Jesus tells us not to judge one another."

"I think I'd better pray about it."

"I ought to talk it over with someone."

"Perhaps it's just a passing thing and will go away by itself."

"I could do no good. All that would happen is that she would resent me bitterly. She'd have every right to."

"It's just not done."

"After all, I could be mistaken."

"I just don't have the time."

Our excuses shrivel before the clear command of Jesus: "If

your brother sins . . . , go and tell him his fault, between you and him alone. If he listens to you, you have gained your brother" (Mt. 18:15).

It was assumed by Jesus that the word *sin* would be equally well understood by both parties. But to go? That is what takes loving courage. What if he slams the door in my face? What if he accuses me of being as big a sinner as himself?

Let us take one step at a time. What is the purpose of your approaching him? "If he listens to you, you have gained your brother." Gained him? Won the argument? Won what exactly? You mean lead him back in triumph to the fold?

You cannot gain or win something or someone unless you first had lost him or had been estranged from him in some manner. Sin destroys fellowship. It is only if we walk in light that we have fellowship one with another. To win a brother is to restore godly fellowship with him. It is that reconciling process by which we smash through the icy wall of estrangement into the warm embrace of fellowship.

Thus the object of going to your brother is to bring about forgiveness and reconciliation. But, you object, there really was no breach in fellowship. I did not condemn him. I was just minding my own business. If he wants to do that sort of thing, *that is his affair.*

Club versus church. Human society versus fellowship in Christ. In the one you can afford to live and let live. Sin is an embarrassment that you cope with expediently. It is not a moral issue but a social inconvenience. But in God's view it is deadly and destroys fellowship.

Take your pick. Do you choose to be a "Christian" club member or a member of the body of Christ? You cannot have it both ways. If you are a member of Christ's body, you go to your brother and seek reconciliation. To say you are not bothered by his sin is to say you have betrayed God's standards and adopted the club's. It is far cozier to be a club member than a member of the body.

But what in the world would I say?

You will say whatever the Holy Spirit gives you to say. Usually it will be short and simple. After all your object in going will be to listen rather than to preach. You cannot condemn without giving Dick a good hearing. It could be, "Listen, Dick, I hear you and Bud have a homosexual relation going between you. I want to hear from your own lips whether it's true or not." After that you may have to make like a broken record. If Dick says, "Who told you? Who's been saying things like that about me?" your answer must be, "Dick, that's not what concerns me. The big question is, Is it true? Is there any truth at all in it? I don't care what other people say. What do *you* say?" From that point almost anything could happen. You may draw a blank. But on the other hand you may open a floodgate through which Dick will pour words of pain, longing, bewilderment and a strong plea for help. Do not forget that God is on your side and that a tussle with the Holy Spirit has already been going on in Dick's heart.

Let me dwell for a little while on the many people engaged in sexual sin who *do* long to talk and to find a helping hand. I personally am at present in the cruelly impossible position of daily refusing to give such help. From many parts of North America come appeals by telephone, by letter, by cable. People even search out my home and invade it at all hours. I am only one man . . . and I cannot handle the flood. *Moreover I have no more to offer than any experienced and godly man.* I can listen. I can explain the Scriptures. I can put perceptive questions at needed intervals. I can point the way to restitution, to forgiveness and to peace. But am I a rarity in this? Where are the thousands of needed counselors for people who are drowning in the sorrows of their own sin or who ache with the loneliness of their alienation from true fellowship? Where, too, are the men with courage to cut boldly into the body of Christ to remove a moral cancer?

Do such counselors have to be professional? Did Paul have a Ph.D. in counseling? What are deacons and elders for? What are officers of Christian organizations for? Is the function of a

Christian leader to lead singing, make announcements and write thank you letters to visiting speakers? We are all playing Christian club games while men and women around us are tormented by sin, too timid to bare their bosoms, too ashamed to ask our help.

Even among those who at first protest (and I have dealt with quite a few) are many who protest too much and break down in an agony of longing.

Several pages back I make the distinction between counseling and disciplinary correction. Not all sinners respond to loving exhortation, and for them discipline is called for. It is a measure alien to Western thinking and abhorrent to our clubby approach to church life. Nevertheless the Scriptures whose verbal inspiration we proudly affirm speak of it explicitly and in detail. We must not play fast and loose with Scripture.

In Matthew 18 a sinister succession of steps is described. If Bill rejects your approach to him, you take two or three others along with you as witnesses. Should their approach meet with rebuff, the approach is made by the church body as a whole. In the event that the church's efforts prove unavailing, *the alienation that in fact already exists becomes explicit in practice.* Temporary excommunication from the fellowship is declared and all church members are called on to carry out the sentence.

We recoil from the passage. It seems to belong to a harsher age, a less "Christian" spirit. Yet ironically the words fall from the lips of the gentle one himself. It is he who gives the instructions. Our discomfort springs from a "kindness" fostered by our culture rather than from a true mercy and love found in the Scriptures. We hate to have the boat rocked.

I refuse to justify the commands of Christ, but I must make one or two comments. First of all, the exercise described in Matthew 18 is a rescue operation from start to finish. It is designed not to condemn but to reconcile. The strange spectacle of family members eating in different rooms of the house has no Scriptural support. If discipline is carried out in the spirit of the deacons who tussled with Andrew and Mary, then the nature of Christ's instructions is being misunderstood. But that is not to say that desperate situations do not call for desperate remedies.

Currently I am engaged in research in delirium tremens, the dangerous mental and physical derangement that occasionally supervenes in heavy drinkers. Several of my patients have become extremely dangerous during their illness. In paranoid rage they have attacked other patients and staff, or have run, practically naked, into the Manitoba snow when temperatures have been around -40° F.

My unit is an "open" unit with no locked doors, and I frown on any forms of mechanical restraint. Yet clearly I cannot allow men in such a condition to do what they like. So I have trained the staff in humane methods of physical (nonmechanical) control, and I also make temporary use of some medications as "chemical straitjackets." My object is to be merciful.

At the height of a delirium, one may not know what is happening to him. He sees and hears things that I can neither see nor hear. He may believe I have a sinister design to molest him homosexually—or even to kill him. Often I can talk to him and calm him, but sometimes he is inaccessible. At that point I must take matters into my own hand and force the issue. He cannot be allowed to do what he wants. He is forcefully restrained and sedated more heavily. Then within a day or two only the haziest recollections of his nightmare remain.

Sin is a far more dangerous and subtle delirium than D. T.'s. To persist in justifying his sin, one must deceive himself about other things. He must create an unreal world around him. It is at this point (since sin is deadlier than delirium tremens) that we must be cruel to be kind. But let us watch our spirits. No punitive glee must ever motivate our disciplinary actions.

Go and Tell Him His Fault

Though I hesitate to comment about the details of Christ's instructions in Matthew 18 (different forms of church government will suggest different interpretations of the passage), I feel we must agree about some general principles. First, one virtue of your private approach to Dick lies in its avoidance of gossip. You went to Dick, not to a committee nor to the prayer group nor to your closest friend. To have gone to any or all of these would have been to spread the dirt around. Had your suspicion of Dick been altogether unfounded you would have succeeded in broadcasting far and wide ungrounded suspicions about him. Christ's method avoids unnecessary gossip. You begin by going right to the source.

Perhaps the doubt still lingers in your mind: Why me though?

Why you? Because your knowledge (or your suspicion) gives you the responsibility. An appeal to someone else could well be a cop-out, a cop-out which would rob you of being used by the Holy Spirit and might damage Dick irreparably. Rule Number One in dealing with sin is to go at the earliest possible moment to the person involved. I cannot stress the principle enough. It is time to go to someone else only when you have failed with Dick.

But it raises yet another principle. Who can forgive sins but God alone? Let us say Dick comes clean. Not only does he admit the bare facts, but takes the blame and tells the whole story (not the eroticism but the inner emotional struggles and attempted self-deception). Let us say that furthermore you both are able to conclude what appropriate steps should be taken: the confrontation of Bud; clear plans to avoid future tempting situations.

You go home with your head in the clouds, praising the Lord. Yet in the night doubts arise. Dick seemed sincere but was he? Ought you not to share the responsibility with someone more senior? And should not some sort of sentence be carried out? Are you, after all, letting Dick off too lightly?

How can you be sure Dick will not fall again? Should a period of testing follow before Dick is allowed back into fellowship? When does trusting God about Dick become naiveté about Dick's sin?

To the questions you ask, ten different Christian leaders would give you as many different answers. Like a distinguished predecessor, I can only give you my opinion and trust that I have the mind of the Lord.

A second passage dealing with discipline, this time discipline specifically over sexual sin, is found in 1 Corinthians 5. But here the situation is far different from the one concerning you and Dick. Dick's was a private thing with Bud. You found out about it by the merest chance. In Corinth the whole church knew what was going on. What is more, *they prided themselves in their broad-minded attitude and actually fostered the sinner's defiant lack of repentance.* Church members in Corinth were all as guilty as the man in question.

Two things follow: The members themselves needed to repent *and* to demonstrate their repentance by the strongest repudiation of the man's sin. By a communal action they were to exclude him from their midst. They were to choose to ally themselves once again with God and to leave the man where his actions had placed him, under the physical domain of Satan.

In the case of you and Dick no such action would be appropriate. In going to him you are declaring that you stand with God in the matter. The action at Corinth involved *the purging of a sinful church* even more than the discipline of an unrepentant man. If both you *and Dick* would feel better consulting someone senior, fine. Otherwise, forget it.

The matter of your responsibility in, as it were, pronouncing Dick clean, is a far more serious one. In the Roman Catholic Church such was the priest's prerogative. In nonconformist churches, where I have had occasion to be involved in disciplinary procedures, a group of the more senior men jointly assume the responsibility of pronouncing the moral leper clean enough to re-enter the camp. The whole business is usually a messy and unsatisfactory one, and I suspect the number of men involved has psychological rather than spiritual reasons. If someone questions the group decision afterwards, any individual can always say, "Yes, I'm inclined to agree. But the rest of the brethren didn't see it that way."

And why should you not, in the name of Christ, and as a representative of his church, be the one to forgive Dick's sin? To whom is the power to bind and loose committed? To Peter alone? Most certainly not. To only the apostles? I doubt it. Compare Matthew 18:18 with 18:19-20. The words of Jesus seem to suggest that there is no elite with the power of forgiveness. Matthew 18:15 declares plainly, "You have gained your brother." There is nothing further to be done. The affair is settled. Should he fall again, that is another matter. But for the present all has been done that needs to be done. To all of us is given this heavenly power of attorney.

Like a fool I have plunged both hands and head into an ecclesiastical hornet's nest, and I am aware of many stinging arguments which could send me howling to plunge in the nearest river. But I must say what I believe to be true. Private sins may be privately dealt with and privately forgiven. Public sins are another matter. Roland Allan and others have written extensively on the subject as it touches the mission field, and it would be inappropriate here to allow myself to be drawn into a major treatise on discipline and authority.

You see my real concern is that we, the churches, *do not care*. We care rather for our reputations. We do not care for sinners. We care for numbers, for buildings, for political prestige, for academic recognition, for the technical excellence of our TV productions, for our growing public respectability. Sixteen-year-old Mary, who has run away from home to have her baby at a clinic while she lives in a hovel, is *only* important if we can feature her in a glossy paper magazine.

God damn us all! We deserve it!

I have for several reasons avoided a more detailed discussion of the group process whereby pressure is brought to bear, however mercifully, upon the unrepentant sinner. There is one aspect of it, however, that I must not leave untouched. It is the one point I have been stressing all along. Group meetings that deal with a sinner are ugly because of the anxiety and guilt we all bring to them.

Instead of our being free to love and to plead, to warn and to rebuke, we are hung up with our own inner problems. We are inhibited. We are ourselves guilt-ridden. ("What will she think of me if I say that?") We are not prepared to lay cards on tables, or to call spades, spades. Consider Jesus at the well with the adulterous woman. Let me substitute here a modern version.

Modern Christian: Why don't you call your husband and come back?

Woman: I have no husband.

Modern Christian: (who knows all the time what the score is): Oh, I see. You're living alone then. How very sad. You must find it lonely.

Woman: Sometimes.

Modern Christian: Don't you ever . . .? Doesn't it ever— well, bother you?

Woman: Doesn't *what* bother me?

I could go on. The dialogue has all the makings of good comedy. But the point is that *love can be every bit as blunt as hostility. We beat around the bush, not because we're tactful, but because we're cowards.* Jesus was blunt because he cared for the woman. He took no masochistic delight in putting her on the spot. Indeed it is clear she did not feel put on the spot. She was merely fascinated by his accuracy.

We approach group discipline with all the hypocrisy with which we conduct our social lives. And because we are not accustomed to being simple, real, loving and direct, we are ill-equipped to deal with real and deadly issues. So we botch it and come away fuming with anger, not knowing why. We feel there should have been no need to "come right out and say it"; so when the time arrives to do just that, we come right out and shout it.

No sinner enjoys being shouted at in the middle of a tense and irate group of people whose frozen smiles flicker into glares of rage from time to time—the misdirected rage of frustrated helpers who know they are botching it and who plainly wish they were a hundred miles away.

So let there be, *please* let there be, in any church group dealing with a recalcitrant sinner, at least one person who can say what has to be said clearly, plainly and briefly.

"John, we have reason to believe you've been robbing the offering plate."

"Mary, we believe you may have been sleeping with the alcoholic whom you're trying to help."

I have touched, perhaps unwisely, on matters of church discipline that are widely debated and on which there is no universal agreement. I have done so because I could hardly talk about the subject of sexual sin and the church and avoid the thorny question of discipline. Yet whatever form the discipline may take, its object must be to heal and to reconcile; and however involved the procedure is, it will never work unless at least one person is prepared to stick his neck out.

In a day of loose moral standards God calls not for mechanical procedures but for people. It was Jesus who approached the woman at the well. It was Paul who so forcefully intervened at Corinth. "Dear brothers," he writes on another occasion, "if a Christian is overcome by some sin, you who are godly should gently and humbly help him back on to the right path, remembering that next time it might be one of you who is in the wrong. Share each other's troubles and problems, and so obey our Lord's command. If anyone thinks he is too great to stoop to this, he is fooling himself" (Gal. 6:1-3, The Living Bible). *Godly*, here, means "on God's side." The process must begin with someone, and if you know of a stumbling sister or brother, it must begin with you.

The principle holds not only for sex, but for every form of

spiritual declension in the day of our public triumph but private failure. The church is a glorious oak, beautiful to behold, but rotten at the core. It cannot be reformed. It must be renewed. It cannot be renewed by structures but by men and women. I can conclude this book in no better way than by reiterating the words of John Howard Yoder. "If [real church discipline is] practiced, it would change the life of churches more fundamentally than has yet been suggested by the currently popular discussions of changing church structures."

It is not too late for the changes to start. The Spirit of God stands by to start them. He will start with you if you are willing to be a focus for renewal.

NOTES

Chapter Three

[1]A. C. Kinsey, W. B. Pomeroy, and C. E. Martin, *Sexual Behaviour in the Human Male* (Philadelphia: W. B. Sanders, 1948).

[2]L. Dearborn, "Autoeroticism" in *The Encyclopedia of Sexual Behaviour* (eds. A. Ellis & Aborbanel) Vol. 1, 204 Hawthorn Books N.Y.

[3]Joel Paris, "The Oedipus Complex: A Critical Re-examination," Canadian Psychiatric Association Journal, 21, No. 3 (1976), 173-179; and Jules Masserman, "The Oedipus Myth" (Paper delivered to the Eastern Psychoanalytic Association Convention, 1976).

[4]Sigmund Freud, *An Outline of Psychoanalysis* (New York: W. W. Norton, 1949), and "Three Essays on the Theory of Sexuality," in *Standard Edition of the Complete Works of Sigmund Freud* (London: Hogarth Press, 1953), IV and V.

[5]I. P. Pavlov, *Conditioned Reflexes* (Oxford: Clarendon Press, 1927).

[6]Donald O. Hebb, *A Textbook of Psychology*, 2nd ed. (Philadelphia: W. B. Sanders, 1966), and B. F. Skinner, *Science & Human Behavior* (New York: Macmillan, 1953).

[7]J. Olds, "Self-Stimulation of the Brain," *Science*, 127 (1958), 315-324.

[8]T. R. Kelly, *A Testament of Devotion* (New York: Harper & Row, 1941), p. 62.

[9]Ibid., p. 39.

Chapter Four

[1]"O Christ in Thee My Soul Hath Found," arranged by "B. E." in *The Believers' Hymn Book*, No. 178 (London: Pickering and Inglis), p. 174.

[2]Wilhelm Reich, *Character Analysis* (New York: Orgone Institute Press, 1949).

Chapter Five

[1]Augustine, The Confessions of St. Augustine, Book III

[2]R. & A. Francoer, *Hot and Cool Sex: Cultures in Conflict* (New York: Harcourt Brace Jovanovich, 1974) and Alex Comfort, *More Joy* (New York: Crown, 1974).

[3]M. Maddocks, *The Atlantic Monthly*, 1973

[4]H. Prosen, R. Martin and M. Prosen, "The Remembered Mother and the Fantasied Mother," *Archives of General Psychiatry*, 27 (1972), 791-794.

Chapter Six

[1]Lionel Ovesey, "The Homosexual Conflict" (Paper delivered to the Association for Psychoanalytic Medicine, New York, November 3, 1953).

[2]I. Berberet, et al., "The Castration Complex," J. Nerv. Ment. Dis. 129:235, 1959.

³I. Berberet, et al., "Homosexuality" a Psychoanalytic Study, (New York: Basic Books, 1962).

⁴Sigmund Freud, *Three Contributions to the Theory of Sex* (New York: N & M Disease Publishing Co., 1930).

⁵Kallman's studies (F. J. Kallman) "A Comparative Twin Study on the Genetic Aspects of Male Homosexuality," J. Nerv. Ment. 115:283, 1962) strongly suggested this might be so, but subsequent evaluations of the studies have called their findings seriously into question.

⁶C. S. Lewis, *The Four Loves* (Glasgow: Fontana Books, 1960), pp. 61-62.

⁷John Donne, *Devotions* (Ann Arbor, Michigan: University of Michigan Press, 1959), pp. 33-34.

⁸Viktor E. Frankl, *The Doctor and the Soul* (New York: Bantam Books, 1967), p. 10.

Chapter Eight

¹John H. Yoder, "Binding and Loosing," *Concern*, February 1967, p. 2.

²Balthaser Humbaier (of Frieberg, 1627), quoted in "On Fraternal Admonition," *Concern*, February 1967, p. 33.